A STRIPPER'S TALE

A STRIPPER'S TAIL

✦

Confessions of a Las Vegas Stripper

Diamond

iUniverse, Inc.

New York Lincoln Shanghai

A STRIPPER'S TAIL
Confessions of a Las Vegas Stripper

Copyright © 2004 by Diamond

iUniverse books may be ordered through booksellers or by contacting:

iUniverse
2021 Pine Lake Road, Suite 100
Lincoln, NE 68512
www.iuniverse.com
1-800-Authors (1-800-288-4677)

Cover Art/Graphics by: Andre L. Hines, New Phaz.com

ISBN: 0-595-33176-9 (pbk)
ISBN: 0-595-66759-7 (cloth)

Printed in the United States of America

I give my family a lot of thanks for all of their help with the children over the years. If it weren't for them, I really don't know what would have happened to the kids and myself. I love my family. They have been great inspirations in my life. They have given me the faith to believe in myself and in everything I do.

To my children, I love you more than life itself. I owe my life to you for keeping me grounded and responsible all those years. I am so proud of you! Always be proud of who you are and where you come from!

Contents

Looking back now, deciding to keep journals of my life as I danced just seemed the right thing to do. I always wondered if anybody else has had my experiences and wondered if anybody would ever care to read. After telling friends my stories they were my encouragement to writing this book.

The stories in this book will be shocking and some will be very disgusting; others will make you laugh and some are just very sad. These are the ups and downs to being an exotic dancer in Las Vegas. Some nights you meet great men who give you a lot of money; other nights you just deal with what you get. Every night is different, and you never know what to expect. That was the fun of the job for me. Every night was always an adventure.

I think at one point or another in every woman's life, she has asked herself the question, "Could I do that?" Anyone can be a dancer with the right attitude. It's fun and allows you to be sexy, sensual, erotic, and for most women, it's a great way to release and escape. The power and the control you have over the men is incredible. It's the kind of power that most women have never had before. Once you feel it, it's in your blood. It is one of the few reasons it's hard to leave the occupation, money would be the number one reason, power and control would be numbers two and three.

Now, before you venture into this, I need to tell you a few things. From here on there will be terms used for the "private parts" of the male and female. I will be referring to the woman's vagina as "cookie" and a man's penis as, "member" or "thing." Stripper lingo, if you will, these are the terms heard most often from dancers while in any club. I just want to clarify what is being talked about or said.

I hope you enjoy this very insightful book about exotic dancers and the industry itself. I enjoyed the years of dancing and enjoyed writing this book even more.

1

How It All Began

Six-inch black platform heels; black fishnet stockings; a long, black tube dress that just barely covers my breasts and my butt, split open all the way to my waist on both sides; long, brunette hair, hanging all the way down my back. The lights are off as I take my place on stage. The music starts, and the lights flash on. I feel the music through every part of my body. I move, and they start to yell and whistle. The louder they get, the more I get into my dance. The power, the control—I don't think I ever felt more in control of my life than at that moment. As I felt the money hitting my body as I lay across the stage floor, I thought to myself, this was it, me at my best. This was my element; this was where I belonged.

It's really hard to figure out when I became interested in stripping. As little girls growing up, my cousins and I used to play around all the time and just always have a lot of fun. Nothing different from what all little girls do. We would dress up and dance. We loved to have parties. I grew up taking all the dance classes and enjoyed dancing very much. I started out with tap dancing, fun but noisy. I tried ballet but found it to be stuffy, and the music could put me to sleep. I decided to try jazz dancing and found my love. The music made you feel so alive; it just made you want to move to the beat.

I had been taking jazz-dancing lessons for almost six years when I spoke with a teacher about wanting to dance professionally. When I was born I had a hip problem, and it has always prevented me from doing the splits. To dance professionally you have to be able to do the splits and hold the position. I have never been able to do the splits. My teacher told me I could never take dance to the next level. I was so upset that I was not going to be able to follow my dream. I wanted to be on Broadway. I wanted to be center stage, to be singing and dancing, doing a job I truly loved. Not too many people are blessed with doing a job they truly love.

I continued on in life and forgot about my dream to dance. I married at a very early age and had two very beautiful children. When I was six months pregnant with my daughter, I walked out on my husband with fifty dollars and a bag of clothes. He had turned into a severe alcoholic. His mental abuse had finally turned physical. I am blessed I have a family that loves me and took me in. I lived with my mother for many years while going back to school to get a degree to support my kids. After graduation I got a job right away working for a developer in my hometown. I worked there for two years, until the job was complete. My boss had purchased land in the Deep South, and they were moving on to build a shopping center. I was asked to move and continue to work for him. Nothing against the south but I don't like humidity. And I really didn't want to move my kids away from my parents. They have been such a big help to me, and it just didn't seem right.

Here I was, unemployed and barely able to make ends meet. If it weren't for living with my mom, the kids and I would have been out on the streets. After a week of looking, a friend referred me to a roofing company that needed a bookkeeper. I went and applied, and

I was working the next day. This job continued for a year. I was not making enough to get a place of my own, and I was struggling to get by. At this point in my life, things seemed really dark. All I could wonder was, "Where was my light at the end of the tunnel?"

I decided to go back to school to get my real estate license. It seemed like a great idea at the time. The town I was living in was booming with growth and the housing market was very good. I went to night school for nine months to learn all the courses. I was prepped and ready to take the state test. My neighbor, who had to take the test three times before he passed, told me, "It's a hard test." I took the test, breezing through it in two and a half hours. I thought there was no way it could be that easy, certain that I had really done something wrong. I got my results three days later and I had *passed*. I was so proud of myself.

Then, of course, another obstacle in my life came when the real estate market took a diving plunge. Interest rates were above twelve percent and nobody was buying or selling. The market was very bad and the best in the business were struggling to survive. Back to square one, I was on a low note at this point in my life. I had just accomplished something I was so proud of and it was basically useless.

Through my life over the years, the two things that held me together were my kids and my Friday nights. There was this great little western bar with a huge wood dance floor. Every Friday night you could find me there, dancing my butt off. I had to release somehow and dancing did it for me. I could swing dance, line dance, hip-hop dance, and rock out. I can fit in with any crowd at any time. I love music and I love to dance even more. From the moment I walked in, guys would line up to dance with me. Not to brag, but I was good. I would walk out at closing time, soaking wet from dancing all-night and loving every minute of it.

It all began when this movie came out about a woman in a custody battle over her daughter and was stripping along the way to make ends meet. I watched her on stage as she did her routine. I was mesmerized. I thought to myself, "I could do that."

It was a month after seeing the movie a friend called and needed a second girl to do a bachelor party. She told me she would give me two hundred for the half hour and tips. We worked the party. I was so scared. I had no idea what I was supposed to do. I had only heard about the girls and what they do at bachelor parties. She told me to wiggle around be cute and slowly take your clothes off. She would take care of the rest.

There are games and other little tricks of the trade that are done at bachelor parties. There is this game called "Whip Cream Races." The dancer takes whip cream and puts it in lines up her legs. The first guy to her stomach got to dive into the "cookie." Of course, all the guys wanted a chance to lick her and maybe get to lick her "cookie." I watched them all line up one right after the other to do the race. They were all licking her one right after the other. That really grossed me out.

Imagine! They were all in line one right after the other. Men are like that and I have never understood it. They will follow each other in line if a woman's "cookie" is involved. The whole game-playing thing was not to my liking, but the money was great. I ended up making four hundred for the half hour. That was easy money but I didn't like the whole bachelor party atmosphere. A week later, I had my friend who took me to the movies take me to the local strip club to check it out. It was this little out of the way bar on the outskirts of town. After I started dancing, I learned that the clubs have to be built in an industrial area, which is why they're built out in the middle of nowhere.

We sat and watched as the girls took their turns on stage. They would dance to two songs. On the second song, they would take their tops off for the last half of the song. Some of the girl's were good on stage, and others had no talent at all. The girls who would do pole work were the ones who made money on stage. When the girls would just dance, the guys would get up and leave. It was really quite interesting to sit and watch.

After an hour of watching, I asked one of the girls to sit with me for a second. I wanted to ask her a couple of questions, so I tipped her twenty dollars for her time and we talked for about ten minutes. I was curious as to how the other dancers receive new girls, if they are really hard on new girls, and how she got started in dancing? She said at the time she was the new girl and the other girls were being pretty good, but she couldn't wait for somebody else to be the new girl. She told me that she was recently divorced and had to pay the bills somehow. I asked her how many girls working in the club were single mothers and she said that most were, but others just do it for the money. She also said that one can average anywhere from three hundred to five hundred dollars a night. I couldn't believe it. It took me a week to make that. Now, I was *really* interested. I wanted to know what I had to do and what the hours were.

The bar opened at noon and closed at two AM. There are two shifts: the day shift and the night shift. Of course, already having a day job, I wanted to work the night shift. I was curious if the manager would hire me without any experience. I figuring that I could do just as good, as some of the girls I saw on stage. I got the nerve up and went down to the club on a Tuesday night to talk to the manager about dancing. He was in the back office when I asked for him. I walked in and asked if I could be a dancer at his club. He looked me up and down and asked, "Do you have experience?" My worst nightmare I was really hoping he wouldn't ask, but without missing a beat I said that I had danced in Reno. I had always heard about the clubs there from friends. So he says, "OK, what's your stage name?" With another split second decision, I offered Diamond because I have always considered myself a diamond in the rough. Finally, when he asked what my body looked like, I pulled my dress up and he said, "You're hired."

We worked it out. I would work Thursday and Friday nights, and in exchange I would work the day shift on the weekends because of my day job. He predicted I would quit my day job within two weeks if I were a good dancer. The money was better than any nine to five job, could ever pull. As a pretty girl, I should do well with the customers.

To tell you a little about myself, I am of German, Italian, and American Indian descent—a very exotic combination, if I do say so myself. I am five-feet-five-inches tall and weigh one hundred fifteen pounds. I have two kids, but lost the weight. I saw that the girls who had bigger breasts were the ones who made the most money, so my first goal after I started dancing was to get breast implants as soon as possible. My own breasts were nice, but I wanted them to look like they did when I was eighteen.

What is really funny to see is the girls who get new breasts and come back with an attitude. Sometimes it was good, but for the most part they have bad attitudes when they come back from getting a boob job. They think they are the bomb, but they are *no* different from when they left; the only difference is that they have bigger boobs. One DJ asked a girl one night if she had paid extra for the attitude she came home with. It should give you some self-esteem, but some girls go way overboard.

My first night was nerve-racking. I was okay out on the floor, talking to the guys and learning the rules of what they call a "table dance." We had to keep a six-inch minimum between the customers and ourselves. We could not touch them at any time. We were not allowed to take our tops off while out on the floor doing a table dance.

The rules were very strict and the girls did everything they could to break them at every given chance. It was quite funny to watch. We would pick our two songs that we wanted to dance to on stage, and that was all there was to it. It all seemed so easy, and yet, that was all there was to making more money than I ever could have dreamed of.

The first time I went on stage, the manager came out to watch. He wanted to see if I was really telling the truth about dancing before. I picked my two songs and headed for the stage. I was so nervous, I couldn't even hold onto the pole. My hands were sweating badly. But from the moment I walked on stage, all the lights were on me and I never felt so alive. I don't think I ever felt that way before. The rush that went through my body was so incredible, feeling that I finally found what I had been looking for all of my life. I am a very creative person and dancing allowed me to express myself. Taking my clothes off made it more fun.

I could dance fast or slow. I could crawl on the ground and be the seductress, or play the role of the fun girl next door. Whatever role you choose to play, they watch. I finally knew I found a job I could truly enjoy and make great money doing it. By the time I walked off stage, I was in a full sweat, both from the rush and from waiting to see what the manager thought of me on stage. I guess I faked it really well because nobody knew it was my first time. The adrenaline rush I got being up on stage was so great. I couldn't wait to go on stage again. I wanted to feel that feeling again. It was a *Dream* come true I was on stage as the center of attention and I was *good*.

Stripping is the first and only job for which I have ever shown up an hour and a half early. I liked to go in early on the weekends and practice on the pole. Pole work brought the big tips on stage, and putting on a performance was what I wanted to do. The manager was right; my day job lasted two weeks and I started dancing full time. That gave me more time to perfect my stage routine and to really put my heart and soul into my performance.

That is how it all began!

2

Learning to Be a Stripper

The very first thing you must do when wanting to be a stripper is to pick out a good name. You need to pick one that fits you and your personality. Here is a list of some of the more common names I have heard over the years. Some are good; others are just, well, tacky. I will leave it up to you to decide: Autumn, Spring, Summer, Sunshine, Rain, Snow, Sherry, Cherry, Cherish, Sweetie, Sweet Chocolate, Chocolate, Cinnamon, Cocoa, Champagne, Peaches, Cream, Sugar, Pepper, Peppermint, Brea, Jasmine, Ginger, Flower, Daisy, Orchid, Butterfly, Asia, Africa, China, Comet, Gem, Italia, Ice, Jewels, Silver, Diamond, Crystal, Platinum, Sapphire, Star, Secret, Sterling, Pleasure, Treasure, Present, Brook, Cali, Cami, Cameo, Chance, Chase, Coral, Dana, Destiny, Heaven, Marilyn, Misty, Mindy, Miracle, Magic, Monet, Mystere, Mystique, Laney, Lucky, Lola, Baby, Blade, Blaze, Brandy, Bianca, Blanca, Candy, Mandy, Randy, Rhonda, Austin, Avalon, Boston, Catalina, Dallas, Hampton, Houston, Vegas, Manhattan, Reno, Rio, Sahara, Savannah, Sierra, Texas, Janice, Jessie, Jocelyn, Wendy, Odessey, Jodessey, Carmen, Candace, Carla, Carly, Chanel, Nikki, Pamela, Ebony, Ivory, Raven, Rage, Adrien, Amber, Angel, April, May, June, Mink, Sadie, Sage, Satin, Silk, Lace, Lacey, Macey, Stacy, Tracy, Tina, Tia, Tally, Lena, Lindsay, Lisa, Jupiter, Venus, Sky, Skyler, Tyler, Taylor, Justice, Felony, Fawn, Tawny, Bambi, Bear, Koala, Tammy,

Thumper, Thunder, Tiger, Kitten, Kitty, Cat, Blonde, Goldie, Pink, Blue, Rosa, Rose, Rosie, Sandra, Sarah, Scarlet, Sophia, Sophie, Cari, Kristen, Krissy, Alex, Alexander, Alexandria, AJ, BJ, CJ, DJ, TJ, JC, KC, Danny, Denny, Dior, Kendall, Kennedy, Frankie, Holden, Joey, Johnny, Reagan, Sammy, Stevie, Teddy, Tommy, Tara, Kori, Torrie, Torrance, Darrion, Destry, Dustin, Camden, Cameron, Mallory, Miranda, Meisha, Victoria, Sabrina, Brittany, Tiffany, Morgan, Porscha, Mercedes, Alexis, Lexus, Lexy, Tasha, Sasha, Valentine and Vixon. I think you get the idea. Then you have Blonde, Brunette and Red Head, and African-American and Asian versions of every name listed.

But please pick a name that fits you, and try to be original. I know it's hard, but it's better for you so the customers don't get you confused with the other girls. The more original the name is, the better.

First and foremost, being the new girl on the block took a little getting used to. Instantly, the girls looked at me as a threat to their money. There are very few dancers I would even want as my friend, so for the most part I kept to myself. I don't like a lot of people knowing my business. Some of the girls were very nice right off the bat. Some were willing to give me pointers on stage while others just gave dirty looks. After being there a month, another girl was hired and they focused on her. She was a horrible dancer and had no figure, so they had lots to talk about. The girls can be so catty.

They can be very mean and very hurtful. They want to chase competitors out of their club because the competition takes money from them. Like I said if a new dancer is a threat to their money they have issues with that person. I am a strong Karma person and I believe in giving everyone that first chance. After that, how I feel about someone is in how she treats and respects me. Not too many dancers even have respect for themselves, let alone anyone else. That is why in my years of dancing I have one girlfriend I know I can trust.

I was very lucky in that dancing came very natural to me, as did flirting. The job was *perfect* for me. There are a lot of things to learn to be a great stripper. Among these are the walk, how you carry yourself as you walk across the room, and of course the all-important great personality. Amazingly enough you don't have to be drop dead gorgeous or even a good dancer; personality will take you further in this business then anything else.

To get used to being in front of a crowd, I had a girlfriend who would do these stag parties once a month at a club. They would cook awesome food, watch movies, and just sit around talking. When dinner was done, we girls would run out, climb on the tables, and start stripping. The guys would give you ones and other bills if they liked you. They would pay us four hundred just to be there, and we would make another two or three hundred in tips. This was a good way to get used to the whole crowd issue. Being in a g-string in front of a couple hundred people will make one lose any shyness she might have. Some of the girls would go completely nude. Others would sit on the guys' faces for money. One right after another, they would try to lick the girls. What would make a man want to follow another man? When it comes to being with women, why would a guy want to put his tongue or face where some other guy just had his? I wish somebody could explain this part of men's behavior to me.

The first thing for me to conquer was my stage performance. I already had the walk in heels and have always been able to carry myself in any room. I went to work an hour and a half early every-day so I could practice on stage without any one there, so that if I fell or did something stupid, there was no one there to see it. I had the DJ show me how to turn on the music and I would just dance and practice my moves. It was amazing the first time I grabbed the pole and lifted myself upside-down, locked my legs, and let go with my hands. I felt like I was back in grade school playing on the monkey bars. I learned how to hang upside-down and spin my way down to the ground without using my hands. It looked beautiful with my long hair. I learned how to be graceful and my stage performance was quite sexy and entertaining. Some girls (like myself) really do take pride in their stage performance. Others just smash their boobs into the customer's faces for a dollar. When I was on stage, I would tell the guys to throw their dollars on stage if they liked the performance. Sometimes the guys would get mad, but for the most part the guys would toss their dollars on stage. I just never thought it to be too classy to smash your boobs into some stranger's face for a dollar.

Once I had some money put away, that's when I began to purchase my outfits or some call costumes. It used to be hard to find good stripper clothes, but finally stores realized what a market there was for the hot shorts and thongs. You will notice when you enter a club that some of the girls wear real costumes while others just wear their underwear and bra. This makes girls look cheap and desperate. Please spend a few extra bucks and buy an actual costume. The prices can range from thirty dollars an outfit to over two hundred for a full-length gown. The hooker shoes used to be even harder to find. Now stores all over sell everything, from regular heels to platforms with heels to boots with heels and add the platforms to those, too. You can take any dancer and add anywhere from three to seven inches to her height, depending on what shoes she wears.

Put the outfit together with the stage performance and you are almost a stripper. The next thing to learn is how to talk to the customers. I have been doing this for some time now and have learned over the years there are only a couple of things you really need to keep up with and you can have the greatest conversation with any man. First off, *all* men like sports. I have found very few that don't have a favorite sport. Personally, I like extreme sports the best. But I would say, it would be a toss up between football and basketball as men's two favorites. If you keep up on team scores or even watch the game right before work, you really will have a lot to talk about. Keeping up with events from around the world is also good, but the most important one of all is that men love to talk about themselves. Very egotistical, but they do. If they are successful in business, they love to talk about it.

I also learned over the years how to judge men and if they have money. I have worked in some pretty rough clubs over the years, but when I finally got to the top I knew how to read men (you should by the time you get to Vegas). This is a secret I really shouldn't give out, but I will. Men who have money don't usually flaunt it. Men with class and style show it in the way they dress without realizing it. Men with money like to wear nice watches. Not a lot of jewelry such as gold around the neck, but they love nice watches. The watch is always an easy place to see on any man as they walk by, or as simple as asking for the time. Men who have money also like to wear expensive shoes, too. Shoes can be a sure giveaway. These are two of my personal secrets on how to read a man as he walks through the club doors. Another way to get good paying customers is to weed out the guys who are alone, or the guys who look lonely. It's easy to pick out the lonely guys and they make great targets for us aggressive dancers; they don't know how to say no. Or the guys who say they have never been there before can usually be easy targets for the VIP room.

I couldn't believe it could be so simple, and the more I ask for, the more they are willing to give. I found that if I expect them to tip me, they don't. I always have to tell them how much they owe and add on a tip. It seems to work. I was always told to ask for what I want; the worst thing that can happen is they don't tip. That is what usually happens, so if you ask, sometimes the guys will give. To all the men who read this, *please* tip your dancer for a job well done.

Over the next couple of years, I had perfected my routine on stage—how to talk, walk, and everything else needed to be a great stripper. Now I just needed a better venue to dance. Somewhere my talent would be appreciated. That's when one of the girls asked; if I was interested in dancing in Las Vegas. She told me about the clubs and the customers and how they have a lot more money. I was willing to try anything to get out of the little town in which I lived. The thought of more money really interested me. My kids are getting older and college isn't getting any cheaper. We made our way to Las Vegas. To get a job in this town, you must first go to the club where you want to dance and be hired. They give you some paperwork to fill out and then you must get what they call a "sheriff's card." Every person in this town has to have one of these cards to work. Some are gaming cards; others like mine are non-gaming. They do a FBI background check to see if you have been arrested before. They fingerprint you and take your picture for your work card.

You give your work card to the bar you are working for. They keep it until you quit or they fire you. It takes four to six hours to complete the process. The girl I came over with almost didn't get her work card. She had been arrested for shoplifting when she was nineteen. They looked at her and decided that since it had been six years earlier, they would let her have her work card. If you have been convicted of a felony, or simply have a criminal background, you won't get a work card in Las Vegas. Take that into consideration before hopping on a plane and flying to Vegas to be a stripper. Background checks are done and you could waste your time coming here if you have a criminal history. Most clubs in most states require you to have a business license to work, as well.

When first starting to dance, learning the rules of tip out are very important. The more you tip the manager and the DJ, the more they like you and respect you. If you try to walk out on tip out, you will be fired. Most clubs want a base rate for you to work the shift. If you don't want to do stage, you have to buy your way off. That can get very expensive by the end of the night. Some clubs charge as much as two hundred to work their night shift; others are roughly forty to one hundred eighty dollars per night shift. Then you have to tip out your DJ, regardless of whether you go on stage or not.

Dancing in Las Vegas is a lot different than where I come from. The dances are more close and personal, and you can touch the guys. It goes from a table dance to a lap dance. There is lots of bumping and grinding going on in the Vegas clubs. My thought was, "If the guy didn't get hard in his pants then I wasn't doing my job properly." I would get offended if the guy didn't get hard. Rarely will that happen, usually after the guy has had way too much to drink. They can't touch you but you can be all over them, meaning you can smash your beasts into their faces, rub your breasts up and down on their member. You can crawl right up on the chairs and put your "cookie" in the guy's face. Some of the girls do a roll up on the guy, so their butts are in the guys face with their legs locked around his head. I personally am not into stripper aerobics. I think it's funny that pole dancing is the new fitness craze. I have never had to work out a day in my life do to dancing five nights a week. How do they think strippers stay in such great shape? It's because all of the dancing. It's the best form of exercise, and fun, too. I get paid to have a lot of fun!

The rules, and the dances, change when you come to Vegas. But then again, *everything* changes when you come to Vegas. Las Vegas is a world all its own.

One thing to watch out for in the clubs is the bouncers. Some of these guys have a mission to try to screw every new girl that walks through the door. I had them hit on me in every club I worked. The bouncers make great money and live in nice homes. Most of the girls would try to date or trap one. The only problem is that most of the guys I knew that worked the clubs had been doing it for years. I would venture to say a good estimate for the number of girls these guys had slept with would range from three hundred to over five hundred. I knew of several bouncers over the years that dated dancers and ended up getting them pregnant and having to take care of them. Some girls have a mission to find a man to take care of them, to give them that nice big house in the suburbs. Some of the guys own up to their responsibilities; others just walk away and leave the dancer to deal with a kid on her own. I watched it happen too many times to count.

Other people to be careful with are the club owners or the managers. Some of them can be sleazy. I worked at a club in Dallas for one day because the manager wanted sexual favors in exchange for me to be one of his girls. When you are the "manager's favorite," you get hooked up with the high rollers who come through the VIP room's back door. Celebrities, politicians, and athletes, people who don't want to be seen by the public. Over the years, I have seen very many famous faces and famous athletes who have visited the clubs where I worked. Some are great to dance for, and others can be pigs. They think because they are rich and famous. They can do what they want to whom they want at any time. Personally, I preferred not to dance for the rich and famous.

It is a scary world we work in. I was at work one night dancing for a group of guys in town from San Diego for a bachelor party. I danced for the guys for about an hour. They were buying drinks and there were other girls sitting and dancing for some of the other guys. These guys were trying to get me to go party with them at their suite. I told them I wasn't interested and they basically excused me from dancing. They knew there was no way I would go party with them. They wanted party girls. I grabbed my drink and walked away.

About twenty minutes later I started feeling the effects. I had no idea what was going on. I just felt sick and things just felt wrong. I asked to leave work to go back to my hotel room to lie down. The next thing I knew, I was in my room, freaking out, wondering how I had got there and where I had parked my car. I was sweating very badly, and everything started spinning. I was so scared. I was sure I was going to die. I had no idea what those guys had slipped into my drink. The drink had a chemical taste to it, and I set it down after one drink.

I woke up at six in the morning, hanging over the toilet getting sick. There was a pillow and blanket on the floor. I am assuming that is where I slept while I was drugged. It happens all the time in this town and I learned my lesson *quick*. Never take your eyes off of your drink, and never set it down. Sad thing to have to worry about, but in this town the men prey on women like vultures.

This group of guys came in the club one night. It was a father, son, and a few of the son's friends for his twenty-first birthday. Dad was quite friendly from the start. From the moment he walked in the room, he wrapped his arm around my waist and was in my face talking to me. He gave me the money to take his son into the VIP room. We went back, and he was so shy and sweet. Kept his hands at his side and was a perfect, gentlemen. When we were done, I thanked him for being a, gentlemen and we went out to where the group was sitting out on the main floor.

When we got there, the father was instantly on me again, "Did you take good care of my son?" I replied, "Of course, I did!" He said, "You deserve a big tip, but before I tip you, I want to take you into the back myself and have some fun." We proceeded to the VIP room. I was in the middle of the second song when out of nowhere this guy grabs my right boob and squeezes as hard as he can. I was like, "What are you doing?" He says, "I can't help myself. I just had to touch them!" I said, "Don't you know the difference between touching someone and hurting someone?" He started to laugh and said, "I was just having fun." I told him we were done, charged the drunk fool three hundred dollars for two dances, and then demanded a tip for the abuse. He said, "I need some light to see my money." I leaned one of the lights over for him to see. He handed me three one hundred dollar bills and I said, "What about my tip?" He pulls out one bill and asks if it's a twenty. I said yes, he hands it to me. Then he asks if the next bill is a twenty, as well. I said yes, grabbed it, said thanks, and ran out the door to the VIP room. It was a hundred and I could see that, but he couldn't. I figured for the pain he caused me, it was the least he owed me.

I swear I thought he popped my implant. It was sore for three days. If a man pops your implant while you are dancing, you are responsible and they don't have to worry about a thing. You are the one in charge of keeping the man under control, and if they get out of control, the fault falls on you. Not quite fair, but when is life fair?

The only other time I ever had someone lay a hand on me while dancing was when I was dancing for this bachelor. I bent over and the guy next to us stands up real quick and slaps my butt. In an instant reaction, I turned and slapped him back in the face. The fool left a handprint on my butt cheek. Next thing I know, there is a bouncer on this guy in a chokehold, telling this guy they don't allow the customers to disrespect the dancers. If they had a problem with that, then they needed to leave. I have never seen so many men jump up and run out of a club so fast. They knew they were no longer welcome and bolted for the door. We may be strippers but that is no reason to disrespect us.

Here is a story to show you how scary men can be. A friend of mine was working the floor when she approached this guy sitting against the wall. She introduced herself and asked if he would like a dance. The guy said yes, but with one condition: "You can dance for me, but you must stand in front of me and not touch me." She thought for a moment and said, "Yes." The next song started and she did the dance. It's very hard to dance for someone who doesn't want you to touch them. There are only so many moves you can do.

When she was done, as she went to get her money he grabbed her hand, pulled her close, and whispered, "I want to slice your neck open and masturbate all over your face as you bleed to death." She screamed and ran for the back. She told the manager what the guy said and had the guy kicked out. She was so freaked out. She couldn't work anymore that night and was afraid to go home because she lived alone. I later heard from another friend she had gone and stayed the night with some friends.

Here are a couple of sad stories that happened to dancers I have known over the years.

There was this beautiful dancer who was a manager's favorite. She was stunning: long, black red hair, with the most gorgeous blue eyes you have ever seen. She had so much personality and the body to match the beauty. She was dancing for a couple of guys in the VIP room, and they got her quite drunk. After she was done dancing for these guys, she decided to leave and head home. These guys talked to her all night and found out she lived alone with her dog. They asked personal questions about her life and found out what they wanted to know.

They waited for her to leave that night and followed her home. She lived in an apartment complex that was not gated and had no security. The two guys jumped her as she got out of her car, and dragged her to her apartment at gunpoint. When they entered the apartment, her dog started barking and wouldn't stop. They took her dog and strangled the little thing. Then they both took their turns raping her at gunpoint for the next five hours.

I couldn't believe the story when it was told to me. I could not imagine going through what she went through. Not only did they violate her, but they killed her dog, too. The guys were never caught. They paid cash at the bar so there was no receipt to follow up on. They knew what they were doing from the moment they entered the bar. You have to be extremely careful about giving out too much information to these guys. They may seem harmless, but they are not.

Another girl left with a limo full of guys and paid the ultimate price. She was hooked up in the club with this group and they offered her more money to go with them and party in the limo. Because she was set up with these guys, she assumed that they were okay and were good guys. Never assume anything in this town. They got her into the limo and all nine of the guy's gang raped her for hours and then dumped her back off behind the club.

This next story goes a little bit further than the last. There are girls that come to dance in Vegas from all around the world. Customers have their pick from over one hundred girls on any given night at any club. These girls are from ten to fifteen different countries. American money is worth more around the world. In some countries, it's worth a lot more. Some of the girl's get work cards to come here for three to four years. They send all their money back home to support their families.

With that said, here goes the next story. I had a friend who came to dance here from Brazil. She loved it so much that she called a couple more of her friends back home and told them about the great success she was having in Vegas. Her friends decided to come join her in Vegas and dance. One of the girls liked to go out clubbing every night. She met this guy and fell head over heels in love with him.

They moved in together within a week of meeting. She still danced, but this guy would sit in the club and watch her to make sure she wasn't doing anything nasty or anything he thought was inappropriate. He was very possessive of her and wanted to know what she was doing every minute of the day. If he couldn't find her, or she wouldn't answer her cell phone, he would freak out. One night, they had a real bad argument and she left for work. He waited for her to leave after the night was done and followed her.

She and a couple friends decided to go clubbing to take her mind off of the argument and the long night she just had. On her way home from the club, he pulled up next to her on the freeway and got her to pull over to talk to him. He grabbed her, shoved her into his car and sped off. Nobody heard from her for a week, and then two weeks. We were all so scared and worried. Her friends called the police and they took all the information, but there was no proof of foul play. The cops found her car at the mall a month later. This guy went back for her car and was driving it around.

When they found her car, it had his prints all over it but no body. It was four months later we heard the news that a female body had been found out in the desert and they were conducting DNA tests. A month later, through the other girls at work, I learned it was her body. They had all flown back to Brazil for her funeral. It was very sad. She was a beautiful young girl. That is why I say you have to be so careful in this town. The men are literally like vultures.

I knew a couple of girls who came to Vegas to dance and loved it so much that they moved here within a month. They got involved with the guys who came into the bar. They started doing drugs and then the next thing you know they were skinny and looked anorexic. They had body acne, which usually means one is doing some kind of chemical substance. They were warned at work to quit the drugs or be fired. A month later, I heard through the rumor mill that drug dealers ran them out of town. They had gotten themselves in so deep that they owed thousands of dollars. The drug dealers in this town aren't too friendly and have no use for a stripper who is strung out on crank or coke and can't pay for their habit. Some get chased out of town; others get found dead in allies or the desert.

What really grosses me out is; the men who hang out in strip clubs so they can have a dancer as a girlfriend. Usually, these men are lazy and don't want to get a real job. They date a stripper for her money and most dancers accept this. I have never understood it, but half of the girls that dance support their men. I hear so many of the girls on their cell phones arguing with these guys. Then they complain that their mood has been ruined and now can't work, or they sit in the back and cry all night. Some of these guy's have good jobs, but for the most part the girls are the ones paying the bills. These guys have pathetic jobs that don't pay anything and the girls are like, "But he loves me." Of course, he loves you; you take care of him. I think these men are just looking for a mother figure and not a real woman. But then again, it doesn't say much for the girls. They put up with it and continue to support these guys.

One night I walked up to this guy and asked him for a dance. He asked me to sit for a moment and then he would get a dance. I sat and we started talking. Come to find out, this guy is an accountant. Has a great job and owns his house. The man was beautiful. He was Italian and had very black hair and dark black eyes. I thought to myself, "This is the type of man I would love to meet and date."

Responsible, intelligent, and handsome—this is the type of man I like. As I talked to him, I found myself more and more interested in him.

As the night went by, he started to get a buzz and told me that he likes to gamble. That was instantly a red flag to me. I have been through that with a couple of my friends and I am not going to go through it with a man. There is no way of telling if this guy is thousands of dollars in debt, or if his house is mortgaged to the max. He tells me about one night he went on a spending spree and had spent $25,000 *in one night.* He had a friend who had spent *$300,000* in three days. I can't believe these people. Here I struggled to raise two kids on my own and they can just throw their money away. I can understand gambling like that if you can afford it, but it didn't sound like he could.

It's really is a strange world to be involved in. There are so many aspects to dancers. Some do it to pay for school; others, like me, had schooling but don't care for the eight to five thing. Plus, you really can't beat the money. Others do it for their drug habit, or to support their useless boyfriends. Some send money home to foreign countries to support their families. Others aren't capable of holding down a regular job.

The money in Las Vegas is *incredible.* The first weekend I worked here, I made $2,500 in three days. That is insane money for three days of work. I couldn't believe I could make that much. I started traveling to Vegas to dance twice a month and then three times a month. That lasted for three months.

3

Making the Move to Vegas

I was getting tired of going back and forth and missing my kids. It was a three-hour drive to Vegas from where I lived. I was putting a lot of miles on my car and the drive itself was getting old quick. I would fly, but it is cheaper for me to drive and I like having my car while I am there. It was really hard to be away from my kids. The three of us are very close and have a great little family unit. I asked the kids to go over and visit with me and check it out. They were willing to try it for a year to see if they liked the school and kids. Well, it's been years now and they still love it.

Moving out here was something else. To move out of state, the trucking companies charge you by weight. I had a small house of furniture to move and it still cost $2,500. I moved into an apartment at first. I wasn't sure what part of town to move to. I wanted good schools and a nice quiet area. It had to be a safe area, that's very important as a single parent.

There are four really great areas in Las Vegas: the west side of Vegas, which include Summerlin and Southern Highlands, and the east side of Vegas, which is called Seven Hills and Green Valley Area. They are all really beautiful areas, but I really fell in love with the Northwest. I stayed in my apartment for a year. Then I moved into a house I rented for another year. It took me two years to come up with a large enough down-payment on my first house. After two years of living in Vegas, I bought my first house. To finally own a house was a big accomplishment for me—another reason to be proud of myself and of the job I do.

After we moved to Las Vegas, I showed the kids the club where I worked and basically explained my job to them. I am not ashamed of the job I do, nor do I want my kids to be ashamed of me. They love their mother. They know I do it for them so we can have a nice house. They have everything they need all the time and lack for nothing. They know I love them and that is all that matters. I don't think they fully understand what I do, but they know enough. As they grew older and understood more, they accepted the reason I danced and completely accepted my job.

Another reason why I left home and never looked back was that a guy stalked me. He would follow me home a little further every night until he followed me all the way home. He found out where I was living and knew I had kids. That is a very scary situation. Vegas is a large town and most of the guys you dance for come from another state. Some are here on work; others to party or gamble. Either way, it is mostly tourists we dance for. Back home, you relied on regulars to come in and see you. It's really freaky to dance for the same guy week after week. They always want to date you. They are just creepy.

The thing I really like about dancing in Vegas is that because there are so many girls, you just blend in with the crowd and don't stand out, unless you want to. At my club back home, everybody knew who you were. When only fourteen girls in town strip, everybody knows who you are. It's nice to just blend in and have a life. You do have to be very careful here, too. Men will approach you all the time and you never know what their intentions are.

Grocery shopping, playing slots at a casino, or even just walking through a casino, I have men come up to me and ask me to gamble with them. They hit on me everywhere, twenty-four hours a day. My son used to get very upset when a man would approach us in a store and ask for my name or number. He used to get very offended by it. He is older now and he isn't so bad, but he used to be very protective over his mother. I had one guy who really upset me, and my son threatened to beat him up. How adorable is that? It just shows he loves his mother.

One year I took my kids to Hawaii for summer vacation. We were tired of just the beach scene, so we decided to buy equipment to go snorkeling. We purchased the equipment, rented a car, and drove to the north side of the island. There is this great bay there everybody goes to snorkel. My kids had never been snorkeling before and it was going to be fun teaching them. We were out there about twenty minutes, having the time of our lives, when all of a sudden out of nowhere I feel this pinch on my butt. I swear I thought a fish had bit my butt.

I jumped out of the water screaming, thinking there was a shark in the water. To turn and find this foreign guy standing there, with a huge smile on his face, made me so mad. I went off on him. I couldn't believe he thought it to be okay to swim up to someone from behind and pinch her butt. I told him that I didn't know what country he was from, but in America that was totally unacceptable. Here I am cursing this man out, while the entire time my son is in the water behind me pointing at this guy and laughing. It has got to be one of the most awkward moments in my life. Had I been on dry land, I would have shown this guy what kickboxing classes do for a woman.

A lot of dancers have a bad attitude towards men. Women get this way because of the way we are treated everyday of our lives by men. A lot of dancers are lesbian and proud of it. But I have also seen some girls fall into the ring of prostitution because they figure they have been with enough guys for free. So they think, "to charge to sleep with me is no different than them taking me for all my money." I guess it's more of a revenge thing than just losing one's morals.

The one thing I don't like is when you need money and you go to work and the men can read your body language without you (or them) even knowing it. If you are desperate for money, you will not make it. It's as if you have a "desperate" sign tattooed across your forehead and nobody wants to touch you. If you don't feel it, you shouldn't go to work that night. One thing you can't do in this business is "fake it." The guys can read the body language, and they can see it in your eyes. Whether they know it or not, guys will pick up on your bad mood and they will avoid you like the plague.

Vegas is the kind of town where anything goes, and it usually does. I have met some really great people, but then again I have met some freaks. It takes all kinds to make up this crazy town. Everybody in this town seems to be after the mighty dollar. A friend of mine is a hooker. I was shocked to find this out. I knew her for a year before she admitted to me what she does. She originally told me she had an adult Web site. I assumed she was using a web cam, but I was wrong.

Men would contact her through the site and she does background checks on them. They set up a date for when they come to town. She will meet them at their room, or sometimes if the customer is a long-time client, she will let them come to her house. She charges

$500 per hour and gives discounts to return customers. I could not believe this is what she did. I had no idea when I moved here that prostitution was such a big game in this town. There are brothels about an hour from Vegas. The cab drivers and the limo drivers love guys who want to go out there. They get paid to sit and wait. Then they also get a tip from the hooker the guy sees. They always kick back. In this town, there is always a kick back to someone for something. It is also a big tipping town, since everyone lives off of tips.

Tipping will get you everywhere. Want to be in the front of any line? Kick out a Benjamin. One hundred dollars will usually get you to the front of any line. Women, all you have to do is look good. Every club wants beautiful women in it. This draws more men and more talk. They love it when the dancers all come out at night for the after hours. The after hour parties start at five in the morning and usually last until noon. That's when everyone crawls out of the bar and into bed, sleeps during the day, and returns to do it all again the next night. Living in Vegas can be a vicious cycle. You have to be strong to make it in this town.

The greatest part about moving to Vegas was moving up to the nicer clubs, and then to the multi-million dollar clubs of Vegas. When you get to Vegas, you learn to appreciate what you have. Well, some do. You can never go back to the little clubs again. The way you are treated, the amenities for the girls, *everything* is better.

4

Sin City at its Best

When reading this chapter, please keep in mind I have danced in every dance club in Vegas and around the United States and Japan. There are some clubs that are the class of the class. Then there are those that are the low of the low. Some clubs make great money because of reputation others have bad reputations. Depending on the club you chose to visit will depend on the level of fun you will have.

I always kept a journal of my life, and dancing just seemed to be another chapter to write about. It was after reading my journals years later that I decided to write about my stories. I have been dancing for a lot of years and this covers all of the clubs I worked in. It was a lot of hard work over the beginning years. I love my life now and would never change the fact I danced because it got me everything I have today. I would never put dancing down in any way. I loved the job and the money I could make as a single parent.

After working in Vegas for a while, I got to where if a customer would pay me to go gambling or out to dinner, I would go. It just amazes me how many men are willing to pay to have a beautiful woman on their arm for dinner and a show, or just to gamble and have drinks. They are willing to pay a lot, too.

The first year I started working here was incredible. That's when I learned how well I could live being a stripper. Every December in

Vegas is the rodeo. You have 200,000 people come to town for this. It's a big thing here every year. The most money I ever made was $10,000 in three days from a guy who was here sponsoring a bull rider for the rodeo. He came into the club three nights in a row and spent $10,000. It was a great Christmas that year.

Around the same time as rodeo, I met this guy. He would pay me money to sit and drink with him. After a couple weeks of this he asked if I would go out to dinner with him. He told me he would pay me $1,000 for the night. No sex, because he knew I didn't do that. I agreed and we went to dinner.

After dinner he asked if I would spend the next night with him again. I told him yes, for another $1,000. We went to hang out at another strip club, because you never hang out at your own club. The girl's just make fun of you and accuse you of being a whore. He loved to watch other girls dance for me. That's what he liked, to watch two women together. I always felt safe going out with him. He didn't want me, he just wanted to see me with another woman. We did the same thing the next night. I love Vegas!

Talking about the same guy, we were out at one of the local strip clubs when he told me he had invited some friends and co-workers to join us. The first couple showed up, they were young and real fun to hang with. Then the second couple showed up and my customer about died when he was introduced to the girl his best friend had brought. The girl said his name before his friend did, but nobody questioned it but me. I was like, "How does she know you?" He leaned over and told me it was a bad situation and we were leaving. We excused ourselves and left. When we got in the cab, I asked, "What was that about?" He started to laugh and just started telling me the story. Every time his guys at work make a big sale, he rewards them with "Head Friday," meaning the guys get a couple of hookers to come into work during lunch and give everybody blow-jobs. It turns out, one of the girls that was a regular at doing this for them was this guy's date. Now the dilemma, does he tell his friend who she is or not? I think he was going to e-mail him her web site.

Working in Vegas can be very seasonal. The summertime brings in lots of bachelor parties, while the wintertime brings in all the conventions. I loved convention season. You could work four to seven days in a row and make anywhere from $2,000 to $5,000, and then take some time off. I learned to work my butt off during this time to save for the summertime when it's not so good. Some years were always better than others; I did great every month because I knew how to work it. You can make money in the worst of times if you know how to work the customers. Dancing for bachelor parties is the absolute worst. You have ten to twenty guys who all have twenty dollars to spend on twenty girls dancing for one guy. Basically, nobody makes money from bachelor parties. Every now and then, the guys will all chip in to send the bachelor to the VIP room, but that's rare. They all want to sit and watch the girls dance for the bachelor. That way, they get a free show. Personally, I would stay away from bachelor parties or would take the bachelor off on our own.

When it's slow, you have to spend a little more time talking than when it's convention's time. During convention season, the guys are there to spend money and they know it. They are in town for three to five nights and plan on having fun for those nights. It's great when you get a guy who likes you and comes back to see you every night they are in town.

When you first enter a club, you will always have a few girls standing at the door. These girls are referred to as, "door whores." Sometimes they make money and sometimes they don't. Most of them don't have any personality and have to rip guys off to make their money. I used to walk the floor and look for my customers, but if I was having a rough night on the floor, I would work the door. Like I said, sometimes it works, sometimes it doesn't. Most of the time, these girls have to get their dances right away. If the guy finds out she has no personality, he doesn't want another dance. Most guys don't fall for it. They like girls who can carry on a conversation. I would make more money off of conversation than dancing. Rich men like women with beauty and brains.

Some men walk into the club and ask if we go completely naked. When the reply is no, they leave. Others will just come right out and ask for what they want. You ask them for a dance and they reply, "Can I suck your breasts?" No! Then the next girl who walks up to them will say the same thing and the reply will be the same from the guy. Then you see her whisper something into his ear and they walk their way to the VIP room. This does happen a lot, unfortunately.

I use to work with a couple of girls who drove up from Hollywood every other weekend. They were trying to make it as actresses and would drive up to Vegas to make money so they could go on their "cattle calls" all week in Hollywood. They would do anything for their money. One gal used to kiss her customers in the VIP room. I wonder if she ever thought about the fact they might have herpes or canker sores in their mouths. Another night, I saw the other gal letting a guy lick her "cookie" out on the floor for twenty dollars a dance. I am sure they were the type trying to make their way in Hollywood by trying to sleep their way to the top. The sad thing is, that's not how the good actresses make it. You have to have more talent than giving guys blowjobs. These girls were young and naïve about life, talked into doing real nasty roles and anything a director or producer might want to get the role. Last I heard, they had both gone into the porn industry.

Relating to the story above, I had this guy ask me to kiss him one night. I told him, "No." He said, "I'm a doctor, I'm clean." I just started to laugh and told him, "Some of the biggest drug addicts I ever met in my life and in this town were doctors." Just because you are a doctor doesn't mean you are clean!

I had so many weird and unusual things happen to me while dancing and living in this town. The biggest thing that makes me laugh is when I go out on the town and see how the women dress while visiting Vegas: shorter skirts than what we wear at the strip club and lace tops with no bras. Do they think they look good? For any women reading this, don't dress up like a hooker while you are here. The locals only laugh at you and it really does look trashy. For those who like to wear skirts with no panties, gross. That is a very dirty and nasty thing to do. There is nothing worse than dancing for some chick and she spreads her legs and has no panties on and expects you to rub on her cookie. I personally don't dance for women unless they are wearing pants. No skirts! I would like to date or know some one better than, "Hi! Want a dance? You expect what?"

Then again, there is this girl I danced with that loves to dance for girls with no panties. She says it turns her on to know she isn't wearing any panties and tries to make the girl wet. She will beg them to go into the VIP room so she can eat the girls "cookie." I have known her to meet customers and their women outside of the bar. She makes a lot more money off of the couple outside of the club. Most women that do come into the club with their men are either bi-curious or looking to hook up with another girl. This other girl I know likes to watch couples screw. They pay her to go party hang out and watch them screw. Whatever floats your boat is what I say. Just when I thought I had heard or seen it all, something new happens that shocks me.

One night a friend of mine was dancing for this girl and her skirt rode up as she was grinding on her. My friend thinks the girl must be wearing fuzzy panties because she can feel them. She turns to me and asks if I can see the gal's panties and what she is wearing. I started to laugh and told her she wasn't wearing any! She turned to find a cookie with razor stubble. Fuzzy panties, that's funny!

While out dancing in some local clubs, I have been witness to some really mind-blowing things. I've seen people snorting cocaine on tables at the bars, people down right screwing in public. Some of the regular dance clubs have private rooms and, if you are willing to pay the price, they will send in hookers, drug dealers, whatever you want. Everything in this town has a price. It's just whether you can afford to pay it or not. Then again, is the price worth it? Drugs can flow feely in this town, not meaning they are free, but very easily accessible to everyone at any given time.

This town can take down the strongest of people if one is not careful. I have seen friends lose everything due to addictions they couldn't keep under control. This town has the means to overindulge every addiction you could possibly think of. That's the challenge to living here, having the will power to fight the temptation that exists all around you everyday. Alcohol, drugs, gambling, sex, you name it, this town can feed any addiction

This dancer got into the Liquid G drug phase. She was so into it, she decided to try to manufacture it on her own. She bought all of the needed ingredients off of the Internet. The site she purchased all of the stuff needed to manufacture the drug also came with complete directions on how to make it. She cooked up a batch on her stove and put it into a water bottle to cool in her refrigerator. After her date that night, they went back to her house to settle down. When she went in to change her clothes, her date helped himself to a bottle of water. She came out to find him passed out on the floor of her kitchen. She dialed emergency and they came to take him to the hospital. He almost died from drinking what he thought was water. She was charged with a bunch of things and pleaded down. She was never seen again.

You can walk into any casino, at any time, and be approached by a hooker or drug dealer. They try to stop the working girls and drug dealers in the casinos, but there are way too many to catch. All you have to do is gamble a little and sit at any bar and the working girls or dealers will approach you. It's really sad how many girls work the casinos. You can make great money being a dancer and not have sex with these men. They charge any where from $300-500 an hour. That's roughly the same money I make for an hour in any club's VIP room, and I am not having sex with them.

There are a lot of escort services and massage parlors here. You call them up and they send out a dancer of your choice. You then work your own deal once they are in your room. Some only dance; others will do anything for the right price. There are legit dance companies and then there are the cover-ups for prostitution. This is where the girls have to be extremely careful of undercover police. They set up stings all the time to catch girls soliciting sex. Because of it being legal in the brothels, they try to catch the girls who work the escort services and the massage parlors. The massage parlors will start with an actual massage then ask if you would like them to massage any other body parts for you. You then work out your deal for whatever you want. Hand jobs, blowjobs, intercourse, and anal, anything you want has got a price. You have to be very careful with the girls you do invite into your room. Never let them pour you a drink or you will wake up the next day having been robbed. They will drug you and steal everything or worse, the guy will drug you and rape you. This is why I always found it safer to work in a club with security and protection. When I would go out with a customer, I would never go up to their room alone. I always had a girl friend with me.

One club I worked in fired a girl for running hookers out of the local casino up the street from the club. She would meet the guys in the club and have them pay her there for the hookers. They would get instructions on where to meet the girls. Any shape, flavor, or size, this gal had them working for her. She was making over $10,000 a night from some of these guys setting up their clients with her girls. When the club found out what she was doing, she was fired and never heard from again. I have to tell you, I saw her again four years later working out of a club in Reno.

Let's get to some of my favorite sayings. These are things men have said to me. Some of them are funny; others are just sick. I guess it all depends on your sense of humor. I will just start listing them off.

This one is one of my favorites. It's me being a smart ass and loving every minute of it. I have to set this up. I have never been one to be able to talk dirty, not face-to-face or even over the phone. When a guy asked me to talk dirty to him, this is how I replied, "The other day when I was at home, I ran out and went pee in the gutter. Isn't that dirty?" He didn't think it was funny. I got a kick out of it.

The most common question is, *Can I have your number?* No!

- *Are they real?* Real expensive!

- *How much for a hand job? If "No," I guess a blowjob is out of the question?*

- *Why do you do this?* How many people do you know get paid to drink, dance and get semi-naked? Sounds like fun to me!

- *Are you married?*

- *Do you have any kids?*

- *How many boyfriends do you have?*

- *How many clubs have you danced in?*

- *Do you have a web site? I like jacking off to web sites!*

- *Have you ever done a Porno movie?*

- *You are so beautiful, why don't you model?*

- *Why don't you have some rich man taking care of you?*

- *How much would it cost to get you to my room tonight?*

- *How many wedding proposals do you get a night?*

- *How many guys fall in love with you every night?*

- *What really happens in the VIP room?*

- *Can I lick your "cookie" in the VIP room?*

- *Can I suck your breasts in the VIP room?*

- *Can I stick my finger in your butt?*

- *Are you bi-sexual? Do you like both? Are you a lesbian?*

- *How many men do you have in your life that take care or your needs?*

- *How much money do you make?* Rude! Does anyone ever ask that question of someone they just met? NO!

- This guy walks up to me one night and asks how much a lap dance was. I told him twenty dollars and then he asked if he could shove his finger in my "cookie." I replied, "Only if I can shove my fist up your butt!"

- This guy walks up to me one night and starts talking to me. After about five minutes of talking, the guy steps back and said, "I came in her to find a stupid stripper with big boobs to put them in my face. You are not that. You have got to be one of the most intelligent women I have ever met and that is not the fantasy." The man told me I was intimidating. He said, "Beauty and brains, what a scary combination!"

- Then you get the guys that ask, "How are the dances different in the VIP than out on the floor?" I tell them more contact, stronger drinks, and it's more intimate. This guy had enough nerve to ask, "You mean for a hundred bucks, I don't get to penetrate you?" I just walked away.

This story really makes me mad. I hate when guys steal our clothes. They take our outfits and I can only imagine what they do with them. I had this guy in the VIP room and we had been back there for about two hours. We were close to the second hour when he does this thing were he goes real stiff and I could only imagine what just happened. I stood instantly to get dressed, when he grabbed my shorts and shoved my shorts down his pants. I was like, "What are you doing?" He said, "If you want them, go get them." I just cringed, thinking, "You just shoved my shorts down your pants and you want me to stick my hand in there to get them? You can have them. I just made a thousand dollars off of you. I think I can afford to buy another pair." It really made me mad, though. It was my favorite pair. After that happened, I ran out of the VIP room and right into the club owner. He asked, "Where's your shorts?" I said, "You wouldn't believe me if I told you." And the sick part is, I can picture this guy running around his house with my shorts on his head. Or even worse, he might be wearing them.

I found out quickly that it is best to stay home on fight night weekends. That's when a big name fighter comes to town. It brings in a lot of money for Vegas, but the type of people it brings in for the strip clubs is bad. During fight nights, the guys are so wired from the fight they are hard to deal with. I remember years ago during a fight night weekend, a fight broke out in the club and all involved were kicked out. They continued to fight outside when someone pulled a gun and shot off some rounds. That was the last fight weekend I ever worked in this town. The testosterone levels are way too high and the guys are ready to rumble at the drop of a dime. They fight over seats at the clubs, the girls, anything they can pick a fight about, they do. They tend to be very difficult to dance for. You are fighting them off of you like an octopus. It's just not worth their twenty dollars.

Some of the clubs you work in do a thing called a "bachelor dance" or "birthday dance" on stage. It's where the guy sits in a chair and has three to four girls take their tops off and smother him with boobs. Some of the girls decided to take it a few steps further. They would take off the guy's belt, make him get on all fours and whip him. Then they'd ride him around the stage. This stripper working at one of the clubs used to beat the heck out of these guys on stage. There was one night that really stands out to me because the next night the guys came back to the club again. I was dancing for the bachelor in the VIP room when we were all laughing about him getting a "butt whipping" the night before. He jumps up and says, "It's not funny," and drops his pants. He had welts and bruises across his butt. He was getting married the next day and was trying to figure out what to tell his future wife. This guy's butt was black and blue from being whipped the night before. I felt so bad for him. I always wondered what excuse the poor guy came up with for his new wife.

There were these two girls who used to walk around together to get dances. When a customer would tell them no, they would stomp on their feet with their hooker heels. They actually got in trouble for doing it to an undercover cop one night. I think it's funny to see the attitude the girls get when the guys turn them down. Some turn so fast their hair will whip the guy in the face. Others will start to walk off as soon as they hear the word no and not even give the guy a minute to give a reason or an excuse. Guys, once you read this, please just say no and shut up. We don't care for the reason why you don't want a dance. We don't like personal attacks by people who are paying to see us. A dancer doesn't need to know that her breasts aren't large enough or her butt is too wide for you. Just say no and be quiet; don't be rude!

I had regular customers, who would come into the club all the time to see me when I was working. They would tell me their stories of the things that would happen while frequenting other clubs. These two guys were here in town and waiting for me to go on shift. They decided to go to one of the nude clubs up the street from where I was working. They were sitting about ten feet from the stage when the next dancer came out. One of the waitresses told my customers it was a transsexual on stage. They were like, "You mean it's had full surgery and everything?" She said, "Go see for yourself." They went up to the stage, waited for her to come around to them for the tip. When she got to them, they were like, "Oh, my!" They stood up and ran out of the club. They told me, "It didn't look like it's supposed to." They were horrified from what they saw. They have never gone into a nude club again. They were mentally damaged. They said there wasn't enough alcohol in the world to drown out that visual. I am sure there are men out there who have had very successful surgery. This is just one horror story.

Whenever a new club opened in town, I would always send my customers over to see what they were like and then they would come tell me. This customer told me about going into one of the new clubs in town. As he entered, this stunning, young blonde approached him at the door. She was about five foot six inches and weighed about one hundred pounds, with twenty of it being her breasts. She walked up and did the small talk, "Hi. How are you? What's your name?" Then he asks her, "How does the club work with their dancing and VIP room?" She explains to him that she doesn't know how the club works, but here is how she works. One thousand dollars for a blowjob in the VIP room, or three thousand and she would go back to his room and he could do anything he wanted to her. He asks, "You mean anal, oral, anything I want I can do to you?" She smiles and says, "Yes. Want to go play with me?" He ran out of the club. He couldn't believe how forward this little girl was with him. But if she goes back to two or three guy's rooms a week, or a few blow jobs in the VIP room, she is making over $50,000 a month. How insane is that for making money? And it's all cash!

This is a story a good customer of mine told me, I am not sure if I believe it or not, but it is a great story. He was visiting a club out of state with some clients. They were sitting at a booth in the back corner of the club. He sends all of his clients into the VIP rooms with the girls. He is sitting there alone when this hot blonde climbs over the table and into his lap. She starts talking to him and tells him that he is making her really excited and she must dance for him. He agrees and she starts to dance. Instantly, he says, "I was rock hard and the size of my member made it very hard to keep in my pants." She pulls up his shirt and sees the end of his member is sticking out of his pants. She says, "Pay me extra, and I will take care of that for you." He says, "Any amount you want, just do it, *please!*" She slides down under the table and proceeds to undo his pants and give him a blowjob, right there on the spot.

After she was done, she did up his pants but didn't zip them up. She climbs back up on his lap and straddles him with her legs wrapped around his back. She tells him, "She got so wet sucking his member she must have an orgasm of her own." She started to grind on him and he said just the sweat running down her chest and the nasty way she was talking to him got him hard again. When he got hard, his member came out of his pants and right into this chick. Obviously, it was a nude club. He said he screwed her right there in the corner of the club with people walking by. One of his clients came back from the VIP room and sat there and jacked himself off under the table watching him screw this stripper. I asked if he used a condom. He said, "There was no time to put one on." It all happened so fast. She got her money and walked away. I've never in my life ever heard such a story but then again it's almost too good not to be true.

Keeping in with that story, there have been times when I have done a body slide on a customer and you get down to their waste, you can smell the stank from the girl before you. More often than not, the guy just came from a nude bar. Some of these girls can be real nasty and not very clean. If a customer tells me he just came from a nude club, I will not dance for them. They either had this nasty girl grinding her bare "cookie" on them, or they had their hands all up in it. Either way, I just say, "Have a nice night," and walk away.

Here is a story that would really upset me as a mother to hear. I was dancing for this guy one night for about two hours in the VIP room. He said to me, "I want to stay, but I have to go. My son is waiting for me in the car." I was like, "You have got to be kidding? You left your son out in the car for the last two hours we've been in here?" He started laughing and said, "He's not a baby, but not old enough to get in here." The kid was seventeen and had his video game to keep him happy.

Then he proceeds to tell me the kid would do anything he asked at the moment because he had just bought him his first blowjob. This was this kid's step-dad and he bought the kid a blowjob. I hope his mother never finds out that this man, to whom she entrusted her seventeen-year-old, had done this. I was shocked by what he told me. My son was about fourteen at the time and I couldn't even imagine the man in my life doing that. This guy thought it was great.

It's amazing when you get a man away from his wife for a couple days in Vegas how they turn into the biggest pig you could ever imagine. I feel sorry for the women who are married to these fools. This goes back to the guys who want you to kiss them or even more who ask how much to go back to their room. Their wives have no idea they do this in Vegas. They would more than likely divorce these fools if they really knew what happened in Vegas. Sorry, guys! What happens here is not staying here anymore!

One night, I walked up to this guy and he asked me to sit with him. I assumed this was because he was interested in a dance. We talked and I asked him for a dance. He says, "I promised my wife I wouldn't buy any lap dances while I was in town but hold on." He hands his friend a twenty and then asked his friend to buy him a dance. This way, when his wife asks if he bought any dances while in Vegas, his answer can be no and he wasn't lying. That's one of the sneaky ways men get around a lie. They are lying, but don't see it that way when in Vegas. All the rules change when in Vegas.

I had a couple of customers who used to come see me all the time. One of them always reminded me, "When a man wakes up in the morning, the only thing on his mind is to find a woman to touch his penis that day." He said, "Men are like that and it's all we think about." How can he get a woman to touch his penis, today? Sex and food are the only things on a man's mind, and if he tells you different then he is lying! From the age of fifteen, that is all men want (according to them). Food, and to find a woman to touch their penis for that day, is all that goes through a young man's mind. I was so shocked by this statement. But then again, every man to whom I ask that question seems to agree. If they could get a woman to touch their penis everyday, they would.

This story tells of a friend who met a guy in the club one night and decided to talk to him outside of the club. She said that they hit it off instantly. The physical chemistry between them was so magnetic that she just had to see where it could go outside of the club. He was flying out in the morning and she wanted to keep in contact with him. They talked on the phone and e-mailed each other for months. He would fly out to see her and wanted her to see how he lived. That's when they both decided it was time for them to have a weekend together in New York to see if their feelings were real. He booked her a ticket to fly out to New York to see him.

They had the whole weekend planned from the moment the plane touched down. They were both so excited about the weekend and couldn't wait for the date to arrive. Finally, after two months of waiting, the date was here and she was on a plane and on her way to New York. She had never been there and was so excited about seeing this man and getting to explore him and New York at the same time.

From the moment the plane landed, the trip was a nightmare. She landed an hour early and he was not prepared. He was still at home out on the island and it was going to be an hour, at least, before he could get to the airport. She waited for him right inside the terminal. She gets this phone call from him, yelling at her. She is not waiting for him in the right place. She had never been there before and was expected to know where she was supposed to be.

Finally, they meet up, now they have an hour drive to get into the city where they will be staying.

They got into the room and she says, "I need a drink!" He fixes her a drink and then asks if they are going to take a shower together before they head down to Broadway to watch a show. She said, "You should have seen the look on my face when he asked me that. I was like, 'No! I need time to get reacquainted again and I am not jumping into the shower or bed with you right away.' She grabbed her stuff and went into the bathroom and took her shower. She couldn't believe she had been in town for two hours and this guy was wanting, sex instantly. They had only seen each other a few times and had never slept together yet. This was supposed to be their romantic weekend. Yet, his aggressive behavior really disturbed her. He had never shown this side before, at least not around her. She didn't know what to think, so she gave him the benefit of the doubt and wrote it off as nerves.

They walked down to get a cab after she got ready in a record time of forty-five minutes. They approached the cab line and at least twenty people were in line waiting. He gets mad starts to complain about her taking so long to get ready. She says, "I am a stripper and work all night in high heels. I think if we hurry we might be able to walk and get there in time." Without complaining the whole way, she walked it in brand new, vinyl high heels. By the time they got there, her new shoes had cut into her feet. She was in pain and her feet bleeding but forced a smile to try to make this work. Everything was going wrong that could go wrong.

They get their tickets just in the knick of time and have great seats four rows back from the stage. Halfway through the show, they decide to head out and find a restaurant to eat. He says, "We just have to walk a couple of blocks to this really great Italian restaurant." Not knowing her feet were bleeding from her shoes, they proceed to walk to the restaurant.

This man was so ignorant to what was going on right next to him. He was so stressed out over every thing going wrong he wasn't even paying attention to her. And this guys stress level was making everything worse.

They got to the restaurant and it was going to be a two-hour wait to eat. She was starving and hadn't eaten all day because of her flight. They decide to go back to their room and order room service. She begs him to take a cab back to the hotel. He reluctantly said, "Yes." They get back to the room and as soon as the door closes he attacks her and slams her against the wall, kissing her being very rough with her. She pushes him away and screams at him to stop and leave her alone. He then gets major attitude towards her and tells her how ungrateful she has been for everything he has done for her. You have got to be kidding me? All he had done since the moment she got into town was yell at her and cause her pain and she was supposed to be grateful? She was like, "you freak!" She packs her stuff and leaves. Runs down to the cab line and takes a cab back to the airport. She jumped on the first plane in the morning and never talked to the loser again.

He called like thirty or forty times. She never answered the phone and never cared to. The guy was a complete creep. I am glad she got away from him before he could have hurt her. This guy obviously had a temper. These are just some of the things women let men put them through. She was in New York all of twelve hours and never cares to go back.

You can't date guys you meet in the club. First, they are never what they seem and second, they are almost always married in another state. I have never seen a successful marriage or relationship come out of a strip club. Not saying it can't happen, but in this line of work the temptation is great.

Sometimes you get these guys that seem real nice, but are truly hiding who they are. They must have something going on inside to make them feel they need this kind of attention or they are not getting what they need at home. I prefer to dance for married businessmen. They have a wife and a life. They only want the attention of a beautiful woman for the moment. They don't push for a date. They have too much to lose by getting involved. But be careful, women, if your man frequents Vegas and his attitude has changed. I can guarantee there is a woman involved in your man's life. Just watch for the signs, ladies.

Here is a great story. I was out gambling with a customer when I hit a couple jackpots. I was on a roll. The machine was hot. That's when he pops out with, "You hit another jackpot and you have to marry me!" I was like, "I don't want to play anymore." He was so upset that I didn't want to take the chance. Marriage is not an option in my life, and especially to a guy who frequents strip clubs. I mean, does he really think a stripper would marry a guy who visits her on a regular basis and more than likely does it at home, too?

I remember this guy who used to go to clubs all over the states and in Europe. A lot of the girls knew him from all around the world. He had this thing for Asian women with long black hair and they had to be petite. He liked to have two to three girls at a time dancing for him. He would have one grind on his member while the other two were on each side of him with their boobs in his face. If that wasn't working for him, or he's not in the mood for that, he would have two girls dance with each other while one was on his lap grinding him. I always wondered what made this man like Asian women so much. So one day I asked. His reply was that he was brought up very high society and his family or friends would not understand or accept it. He was raised to marry into another wealthy family.

He had gone to school in the Midwest and attended college there, too. He said that his first fling was with this little Korean girl. He loves the Asian women because they will talk dirty to him and will be nasty with him. They pull their thongs aside for him to see and feel their cookies. They like to bend over and show him their butts and let him finger them in the butt while they are dancing for him. One time, I saw him undo his pants and one of the girls stick her hand down his pants and suck his thing in the back corner of the VIP room. They have no problem being nasty for him and to him. He really likes that, but then again what man wouldn't like a women being nasty on him. I mean, heck, *that* is why I have a job. I am not saying that all Asian women are nasty. That was what he said to me. I have danced with many Asian girls over the years and some are very nice. I have friends who use to play the Asian gal, "Twenty dollars me love you long time or at least for one song." The guys loved it.

I have also had guys from the Deep South say the same thing about African-American women. Back home they can't touch. Their friends and family would disown them. So, when they come to Vegas they get to play with the type of girls they can't touch at home. Vegas is the town where if it's taboo, it happens here.

Some of the girls who dance really don't have a lot of morals. The things I have seen girls do for money. Some will do things right in front of you, while others try to hide what they are doing.

There was a girl fired for screwing some guy in the back corner of the VIP room. There have been others who have been caught giving guys blowjobs and a few others over the years that have been caught with their hands down guy's pants giving hand jobs. This one time I saw this girl with her butt backed up to the guys face and the guy was licking her butt and other spots. Like I said, some hide it; others don't care if you see them.

There was this other girl who was one of the manager's favorites, just for the fact that she would let customers finger her. They would just sit and talk the entire time they were in the VIP room and now I know why. She sits on their laps with her butt off to the side with his hand underneath her. She did this all the time. I don't under-stand how girls can let guy's they don't know stick their fingers inside of them. You don't know where his hands have been, and the money in Vegas is very dirty. It could have any number of bacterial infections waiting to take hold. There was another girl who com-plained about how she always had yeast infections and now we know why. Keep the customers fingers out of your cookie.

Talking about the same girl, one night while she was dancing for this guy in the VIP room, she felt something wet between her legs. She wasn't quite sure what it was, but thought maybe the guy had spilt his drink on his leg. She just kept dancing. When the waitress came over to give the man his change from buying their drinks, the light caught something from the corner of her eye. She noticed the stain on his leg was too dark to be any drink he might have spilt. She got up and looked between her legs and noticed she had started her period and rubbed it all up and down this guy's leg. She was horrified. The stain on the guy's pants was from his knee to his pocket. To make matters worse, the guy was wearing khaki pants.

She started to cry and took off running for the dressing room. I was dancing next to her and saw what happened. The guy was actually very cool about the whole situation and felt bad for her. He knew how embarrassed she must have been. He gave me the money he owed her and asked me to please give it to her. She had earned her money and she didn't mean for this to happen. He kind of laughed it off, and then left for the restroom to see if he could get some of it off his pants before he had to go out in public. I felt bad for him having to walk back through his casino with this big stain up one thigh of his pants. I mean it went from his knee to his front pocket. It wasn't a little streak on his leg. I wonder if he had them dry cleaned or if he threw them away?

Here is a great one. I had danced for this guy one night. We did ten dances out on the floor. At twenty a dance, he owed me $200. He reached into his wallet and counted out ten bills to me. I said, "Thank you," and walked away. I went into the back to have a drink of water and rest. When I looked into my purse, the ten bills were all hundreds. He had given me $1,000 instead of $200. Thanks for the *tip*!

I had a girlfriend who used to be able to play guys really well. She could have them depositing money in her bank account from another state. I remember this one man she played for over $15,000. He was married and willing to leave his wife for her but she told him no. She liked being single and leaving his wife would be the worst thing he could do. She also told him she was Catholic and didn't believe in sex before marriage. That's how she got out of not sleeping with him. Religion and the fact that he was already married was an issue for her. It lasted for about six months. All she had to do was call him and say she needed money. He would just go to the bank and put $1,000 at a time in her account. I can't believe the lengths that men will go to see or touch a woman's "cookie." The power of the vagina!

Here is a story that reminds all of us to be careful what we wish for because it just might come true. Her goal of being a dancer was to find a rich man to take care of her. That was all she wanted, to be taken care of. She met this guy from Alabama who owned a marketing business. She started dating him when he came into town. They did this for six months. Then he started flying her back to his place for a week or two at a time. When she got out to his place for the first time, you could imagine her surprise to find out he already has this crank-addict stripper living with him. He plays it up, saying she is down and out and he is helping her. She flies back and forth for a couple of months. In the process, she gets to know this other girl pretty well. Turns out, this guy was lying to her the whole time and he and this gal have been living together for sometime. She has a fit. They get into this huge fight. He swears he will change and they make up and they all go out to party. I was shocked she was letting him get away with this.

She likes to take pills to get real mellow and have fun. Mixing with drugs and alcohol, she was pretty messed up. She had no self-esteem and was willing to tolerate his behavior. He talked her into doing a threesome with the other girl one night. To my surprise, my friend was okay with all of this and rather enjoyed herself. They do it all the time now according to her. She got pregnant and the other girl sleeps in the spare bedroom next to theirs. It lasted for a year after the baby was born. She is now back dancing to support the baby and herself. He pays for the kid, but is very mean to her. She got a lot more than she wished for!

Speaking of taking men for all they can, this girl that I danced with for a while was a real sweet girl. She was very young and beautiful. She had a customer that owned a car dealership. He would come into to town at least once a month to see her and give her money. She came to work one day and told me she met this guy who was Russian and she married him to help him get his green card. The next thing I know, she told me that she was pregnant. I didn't see her for a few months while she has the baby.

When she came back to work, she said, "You won't believe what I told my customer to get him to support me while I was pregnant." She starts in with, "I told him I was artificially inseminated in Miami." I was blown away that this man would even believe this lie. This guy had to be more intelligent than that. He asked, "How it was done?" She told him that they put her to sleep and she didn't know how they did it. All the while, he was sending her $6,000 a month to support her and her new husband while she was pregnant. They had a great honeymoon in Puerto Rico. Then she has this guy's kid and the customer doesn't know to this day he paid for the whole thing. Well, he might know now.

Then I get these guys who come in on a constant basis to see me. They come to town every month or every other month. They are usually great money for a while, then they pull the, "I would love to see you outside of here. I want to date you!" That's when the money is gone and I inform them that I was only nice for the money, and I have no interest in dating them.

There was this time I thought I had a friend in a girl I worked with. I came to find out, she was very jealous of me. She hated the fact I had customers who came to see me from all around the world. She would always try to get my customers to give her money. She would start off with, "Would he buy me a drink?" Then she would wait for me to use the restroom and talk them into letting her dance for them. Not that you had to talk very hard to get these guys to say yes. But there is a Stripper Code that does exist in our world. After the second time she did this to me, got completely hammered, and cost me about a thousand dollars, it was time to kick that relationship to the curb.

Here this girl was on her own, no kids, and basically no responsibilities but a house and car. She would constantly be two to three months behind in her mortgage and would beg her mom to pay her bills or the mortgage company was going to foreclose on her. She would make anywhere from $4,000 to $6,000 a month and could never pay her bills. I could never understand this. Must be a hidden drug problem there, or she is supporting one of those loser boyfriends. How do you make that much money and not be able to pay your bills?

Over the years I have seen a lot of girls come and go. Some make it; others lose out to their addictions. I think a lot of these addictions are due to the lack of self-esteem and because of the way that customers treat dancers on a daily basis. Some use illegal drugs to hide the pain, or from the shame they feel. Others openly admit to being a legal drug addict by doing prescription drugs. Most just drink a lot at work. They will all tell you the same reason for this to be able to deal with the men. So before you know it, they are drinking or popping pills or doing illegal drugs four to five times a week, depending on how often they work. It is a very vicious cycle to get caught up in. I thank God that I have so much more going for me and used dancing for the money and never took anything personal. I never let it get me down. Just keep your eye and mind on the prize: the money to retire, for school or travel, your choice. The world is at your feet if you use the job right.

A lot of these girls work day to day without saving a dime. They don't realize you can't do this forever. Gravity starts to take affect after a while. In this job, you are like a professional athlete; it's only there for so long and then you are forced to quit. Personally, I had to quit do to a knee injury I sustained while in high school. I still go back every now and then to say hi to my friends. I had knee surgery and the doctors are positive that I am going to have severe arthritis due to the dancing in heels and the years of bending. A lot of these girls party hard and it shows by the time they are thirty. They look forty or older from all the drug abuse, late night hours, and just not taking care of themselves. They just don't have a clue what they are doing to their bodies. I hope they all read this and start to take better care of their bodies. I am paying the price and nobody else needs to suffer in pain from something they could have prevented.

Another rule: if a guy tells you don't worry about a thing tonight, I promise I will take care of you, those are the ones who are going to rip you off every time. Lesson learned. Every dancer will learn this lesson as soon as you start dancing. It's really sad when a guy comes into a club with the intentions of ripping off some unsuspecting girl. They will usually walk the entire club talking to all the girls looking for the new girl. The other big scam by guys is walking to the bathroom in the VIP room and exiting out the door instead of using the bathroom. They can only get away with this on an extremely busy night. It doesn't happen that much anymore. A lot of us girls have learned to get our money before they leave the area. Just protects you and them. Some guys get offended when you ask for your money, but once you explain you have been ripped off to many times to count then they understand.

Another big rip off situation involves the girls. I trust no one. The only people I trust with my money are management, and that's only in some clubs. Some management can be just as sleazy as the guys who walk through the doors. Some clubs will not tolerate prostitution out of their clubs and others will let their girls leave with customers as long as they come back and tip out on what extra they earned. I personally chose to dance at clubs where prostitution was frowned upon. You can make just as much money, if not more, just by dancing. You don't have to take it to that level unless you can't dance and it's all you can do to make money. A lot of girls will get mixed up in the porn industry and it's hard to come back once the line has been crossed.

I have a great friend that flies in from New York all the time to work. She really knows how to work the guys. She met this guy while he was here with another stripper from Alaska. She danced for them all night in the VIP room and he gave her $5,000. This guy likes to play with dancers and have them as companions while he does business. He flew the other girl back to Alaska and wanted my friend to fly with him to Chicago and stay with him while on business. Her car had just broken down and he felt sorry for her. He took her out to the Mercedes dealer in New York and paid cash for a new car for her to drive. He had her drive him home and let her keep the car. Whenever he wanted to travel, she would go with him. I was kind of suspicious about the whole thing so I had to ask her,

"Are you sleeping with this guy?" She swore to me she wasn't, but I didn't believe her. Not to many men would give a woman a Mercedes if he weren't getting something in return.

To make a long story short, she moved here to Vegas and stopped taking his calls. He tried to call the car in stolen, but because he let her drive off the car lot in the car, he couldn't. She has been driving around in a brand new Mercedes for the last year. The tags came up on the car and he has the registration, so she has no way of registering the car. She talked to a few dark characters here in town and for the right price it was gone one day. The car was just missing from her driveway. Like I said, everything in Vegas has a price.

This other time, she had customers in from Mexico. They owned timeshares. They were pretty wealthy men. They came into the club one night and she called me over to sit with them. After about an hour of discussion, we decided to leave the club and go gambling. They gave us $600 to leave the club and go gambling with the promise of much more.

We met them over at the casino and they gave us each a $500 Chip to start gambling with. After that was gone, they gave us another chip and asked if we wanted to go have a few drinks. We went up to their room and poured some drinks.

By the time we went back down to gamble, I was so buzzed. I wasn't even able to gamble, but they kept handing me chips. They took us shopping at one of the top scale casinos. They bought me a designer gown and had it altered to fit. The dress itself without alteration, the shoes, and the purse they bought were $800. It was this incredible shade of lavender. We were going to dinner the next night.

Next thing I know, it's eight in the morning and time to go home and try to get some sleep before time to go to dinner. I get a phone call from my friend the next afternoon and dinner is canceled. The guys don't feel good and they will see us the next time they come to town. Thanks for the dress; it's stunning on me. As for all the chips they gave me, when I cashed them out the next day I had over $2,000 in chips. Plus the original $600 they gave us in the club. Let's not forget about the gown either. Not a bad night's work and lots of fun, too.

There is this place in every club that I refer to as "condom corner." Several times I have gone back there with a guy who was sitting with a group of guys and the things that happen back there scare me. I usually don't go there to dance. I got to the point where most guys will take me to the VIP room, because I know how to sell it.

I have seen girls screwing guys back in condom corner. One girl got caught and told the bouncers it was all a misunderstanding. How do you misunderstand a man's penis inside of you at a strip club? I have also seen them, jacking guys off in their pants. Most men will put a condom on so they don't get a big wet spot in their pants. Then they just pull it off and throw it on the floor. Yuck! I had *no* idea this was why they sold condoms to the guys in the bathroom. I had a customer ask me one time when I first started working there why the bathroom attendant offered him a condom. That's the answer to that question. Then you have some guys who are proud of their wet spots. Those are the really sick ones. When that happens while I am dancing, I quit dancing for them and demand my money. Plus a huge tip!

I have many more stories; unfortunately, they aren't suitable for print. I could go on and on about all the crazy things that have happened to me over the years. But I think you have a great idea from these stories what we as dancers really go through every night of our lives. We see the dark side of men. It can be very frustrating, on the other hand it lets me live well. I can't complain too much. It's a rough life, but it can be very rewarding if you use the job and do not let the job use you!

5

Fantasy and Fetish

This is the chapter that will talk about all the strange and weird requests I get from men. There are a couple of stories that are quite unbelievable. Some are really gross and others are really funny. You can never take anything personal. For the most part, the customers are the ones that are drunk and being stupid.

This girl used to find couples at work to go party with and have sex with. Before she settled down and gave up her party life, she used to meet couples in the club and go back to the casino with them. They would party, drink, and screw. Sometimes, it was just the wife or girlfriends; other times, it was both of them. She used to tell me the stories of her and these couples. She said for her to be with both of them, she would charge them $1,000 for the night. That was drinking, dancing in public, and basically putting on a scene for all to watch and envy the guy. If the guy just wanted to watch, it was $750. I asked her where she got her prices. She said it was the price she got the first time she decided to do it. So, she just stayed with the price. She also told me the only way she would be with the man was if he was good looking. She used to make a lot of money by finding couples in the club that wanted to do threesomes. Like I said, they come in all shapes and sizes, and there is someone for every one.

Another girl told me about her and her man having a threesome with a girl they met out at a club. She said her man had been asking her to try it. She really didn't want too, but he begged her to one night. She did and she regretted it from the moment they did it. Now he wants her to bring girls home for him all the time. She finally broke up with him, after four months of tolerating his behavior. I could see doing it if you liked it, but she didn't like it and only did it to make him happy. Well, it made him happy and just made her miserable. Of course it made him happy. Isn't that every man's fantasy?

I had a friend who worked at one of the nicer casinos. He had a friend coming into town for a fight night and wanted to introduce us. I agreed to meet this man because he comes into town on a constant basis and it would be great money. I met him at the casino. We hit it off right from the start. There was definitely a very strong connection. The physical connection was throwing off sparks. He lived out of town, so that made him the perfect customer: rich, intelligent, and great looking, all of the things I look for in a man. I met him at the club the next night. Right away, we were both very comfortable with each other. He was incredible and then the bomb shell, "I'm married!"

It never fails, you meet a good man (what I thought, was a good man) and he is already taken. He came into town to see me for a few months. Then he decides he would like to introduce me to his wife in the hopes of doing a threesome. I was so stunned; *that* was why he was interested in me. He and his wife wanted to have their very own "girlfriend," someone they can take on cruises and on their vacations. After he explained all of this to me, I thought to myself, "What a creep!" Here was this great looking man, who has a nice-looking wife, a beautiful kid, and a great job, and that's not enough for him. He must have a girlfriend on the side, too. I felt sorry for this couple. Here are two people who have so much going for them; they have a great life and they want to live like this.

It shocks me to see people do this to their marriage, when they have everything going for them. It never fails that it almost always ruins the marriage. Jealousy sets in, whether it's the wife or the girl-friend. I have never seen anything good come from adding a third party to any relationship. I can understand a onetime thing with some girl here in Vegas who you know you will never see again. But don't take them home. Keep your private life private and don't take any part of Vegas home with you. That includes a disease!

I have known a few dancers over the years that would pick up on other dancers to take them home to their husbands. They wouldn't join in just bring them home for their man. They either sit and watch, or just go into another room while he is screwing this other girl. One of the dancers and her man go out on the town to find their girl. They try to find a girl who is in town visiting, that way she won't turn into a stalker freak on them. They had one chick here in town give them a lot of trouble, so now they seek out girls from out of town.

One night after work, a friend and I decided to go out dancing after work. We went to one of the local hot spots. Once there, this couple was being very obvious about hitting on my friend. They wanted her to go back up to their suite there at the hotel and party. They were like, "We got some drink, smoke, and we want to go play." She really wanted to go, but was scared to go alone. She begged me to go up, party, and just watch. I said, "Okay," and we followed the couple to their room. They were party animals. They had lots of drugs and lots of alcohol. We sat and partied for a while, and then my girl friend and the guy's wife started to mess around. I just sat in the corner at the table and watched. It was really cool a live porn show. The guy sat in a chair in the corner at the table by me and masturbated for a while and then decided to join in. After a few hours of watching and way too much alcohol, I decided to leave. The couple paid my girl friend $5,000 to stay the weekend and play with them. There are a lot of girls that do this in town.

Or if you don't want to have to bother with trying to pick up on a girl or a couple, there are other ways to see sex shows here in town. There are a couple of hotels where you pay an entrance fee and you have your free reign to walk the halls. Men are not let in alone, and must have a woman with them. They have taken all the doors off of the rooms and the couples can pick any room they choose to have sex in. Then other couples or groups can walk the halls and enter your room to watch. Some ask if you want to participate; others just want you to watch. So you can go in there to have sex, or you can go to just watch.

Another night, I went to meet up with a couple of my good customers to go out to party and have fun. They had already picked up on a couple of other strippers from another bar. These girls were so messed up on drugs. We were all in the front of the bus when one of the guys says, "Hey, everyone, look behind you!" We all turned around to find these two girls completely naked and doing 69 to each other. They continued on for about an hour in the back of the party bus: another free porn show. The guy's were, *loving* it, watching these two girls kissing each other and going down on each other. Then one of the girls pulls out a strap-on. This continued on for another hour. We all just sat there in the bus and watched these two girls going for it. Like I said, "It takes all kinds to make up this town."

Personally, I have always liked boys. It's like when you see a great looking man it can just make you wet and you must have him. I have never had that happen to me over a woman. If I ever saw a woman that made me wet and made me feel that I must have her, then I would, but that has never happened. I have had several friends over the years that tried *believe me,* they tried. When you are both dancing for a guy and they lick you and play with your tits. They aren't doing it for his pleasure. I had one girl tell me that she would like to turn me upside down and lick me from my toes down. Some can be very blunt; others just *stare* at you in the locker rooms while you change. It's kind of creepy when you catch the girls staring.

One night, I met this couple and they wanted me to dance for the wife. They were really nice people and seemed very down to earth. They tell me the story of their first visit to a strip club. She knew her husband went to the clubs while in Vegas. On one trip while she was with him, she asked if she could go see what all the talk was about with regards to the strip clubs. So he agrees to take her, but only if she will be open enough to get a dance. He said, "I created a monster that night." She got into more than he did and fell in love with these two girls that were dancing for them. He said, "That night, my wife turned bi-sexual." They invited the girls back to their room and played with them all night. When they got home from their trip, his wife tattooed these girls on her butt. She put one on each cheek. Now he refers to them as "the girls." It was really quite funny to see these two interact with each other. They really did love each other and enjoyed sharing that part of their life together. I asked why she liked going to the clubs. Her reply was, "Who wouldn't love having a beautiful woman rub her large breasts all over your body? They are much softer and more delicate about the way they touch you. I can see why men love to come to strip clubs so much. The women are *incredible!*" I wish more women had an opinion of dancers like that.

This guy came right up to me in the club one night and asked if I would sit and have a drink with him and listen to his fetish. We ordered a drink so I could listen to what the guy had to say. I am always up for listening; *doing* is another story. He proceeds to tell me he likes to buy women's panties off of the Internet. He said, "The girls masturbate in their panties, then seal them in a plastic bag and send them out for twenty-four hour delivery." He receives them still wet and loves to lick them. His favorite was this gal that would "soak" her panties for him. He said that he had over a hundred pairs. He wanted to know if he could buy mine. I just started laughing and got up and walked away. He has got to be kidding. Women are selling their soiled panties on the Internet and men are buying them? What is the Internet going to be used for next?

This is a good one. I had this guy come up to me one night and asked if I could handle what he wants. I asked him what he wanted and he said his life was very controlled and he wanted someone else to have complete control of him. I asked, "Exactly, what do you want me to do?" He said that he would pay me fifty dollars a dance to slap him, step on him, and kick him while I was dancing for him. I was like, "You have got to be kidding? You are going to pay me fifty dollars a dance to beat the heck out of you while I dance for you?" "Yes," he said. I told him, "Money up front before each dance and I would do it."

Three hundred dollars in and one of my bouncers walks by and saw what I was doing. When he walked over to stop me, I explained that the man was paying me to do this. He just smiled at the bouncer and said, "I really am!" My bouncer just called him "sick" and walked away. This went on for a couple hundred more and then the man asked me to spit on him. That was where I drew the line. I think spitting is gross, let alone *on* someone. Yuck! I think it was pretty cool, though. I got to beat the heck out of this guy and get paid for it. I got to take out my frustrations from every other loser I have ever encountered on this one guy and got paid for it. I'm there.

Sometimes these guys can be too much. I was dancing for this guy in the VIP room and he starts in with this, "Talk dirty to me." We already know what happened the last time someone asked. I just started laughing and asked him what he wanted me to say. His reply was, "Tell me you want to see me suck another man's penis!" I said, "What did you just say?" He said it again, "Tell me you want to see me suck another man's penis!" I stood up and very loudly said, "You want to suck another mans *what?*" The guy turned beet red. I asked him for my money and left him sitting there. I could not believe he said that to me. He was definitely in the wrong bar for what he wanted.

A friend told me about this guy talking dirty to her and telling her that he wanted a vibrator shoved up his butt. These guys really go too far sometimes. I can understand saying something like that to your partner, but not to some stripper you just met. Do you guys really think we want to hear this? No. Or better yet, this guy asked me to pass gas on him. I was so disgusted with this guy. I couldn't believe the guy actually asked me to fart on him. Is there no end to the sickness?

This one goes a little bit farther than the last. I was dancing for this guy out on the main floor. After four hundred dollars worth of dances, he pops out with, "I want a Golden Shower!" I said, "*What* do you want?" He said, "I want you to pee down the front of me for a thousand dollars." I told him that I had problems peeing in a public restroom, let alone *on* someone, but if he gave me $200 and replaced it, I was sure I could find some drunken stripper willing to do it.

I went into the back and said, "Listen up, girls! There is this guy out front who wants a girl to pee down the front of him for a grand." Some of the girls were horrified; others just laughed and said, "What a pervert!" The one I thought would do it stepped up and said, "Point this guy out." Eight of us followed this gal over to where the guy was sitting. We all stood back, but wanted to be close enough to watch. She sat on his lap and they talked for a couple of minutes. That's when we saw him give her the money.

The next song started and she started dancing for this guy. Now you have to picture this. This guy is sitting in a regular chair with arms on it. She slides one foot up both sides of his legs in the chair, and puts her butt on his stomach. She backs her butt up to his chin, pulls her thong aside and we just watched as his shirt soaked. You could see his shirt, go wet from his chest all the way down to his pants. You know the guy was, *loving* every minute of it. You could see his eyes roll back in his head from the thrill he was getting. A couple of the girls gagged and took of running for fear of vomiting. The rest of us stood there and laughed. Sin City at it's best.

This one goes even farther. This guy used to pay a good friend of mine to pee in a glass so he could drink it. He would order a tall drink and go into the bathroom and dump it out. He would then give her the glass to pee in. She would take it into the back and have one of the male bouncers pee in it for her. She would then take it back to her customer for him to drink.

There was this girl who dressed up like a Catholic School girl. She would wear the little plaid skirt with a white top, the white knee-high stockings and the hooker heels. She would pull her hair up into ponytails and put ribbons in it. She was blonde and very cute. They fired her one night because they caught her peeing in one of the chairs out on the dance floor. They kept finding chairs out on the main floor with huge wet spots. It didn't smell like alcohol was being spilt. The waitresses kept an eye on the girls and, lo and behold, she was caught peeing in a chair. Some girls have no class.

Then a friend told me about this guy who use to come into her club and pay three girls $400 each for them to take a box into the bathroom and poop into it. What he did with it they have no idea. But for the $400, they didn't care. How sick is that? I have heard other stories of guys wanting girls to poop on them. They poop on their foreheads and backs. The guys say, "It's the sensation of the heat that's the thrill. Whatever!

Here is another one of those gross requests (not that most of these aren't). A friend was telling me about this regular customer who would come to see her weekly. At the place where she danced, they would go into little booths where there was a glass partition between the dancer and the customer. The girls would strip down completely nude. He would pay her $200 to take any other guy into the booth. The only thing is the guy had to masturbate on the partition separating her from the customer. Then the regular customer would pay her an additional $300 to sit there with him and watch him lick the mess off the glass from the guy before him. Now that's *sick*! Licking spit off a New York sidewalk would be cleaner than that!

Then you get the guys who want to pay to see two girls go down on each other. For the most part, the girls can get away with it, but they do get told to keep it "discrete." There are a couple of girls famous for this and the funny thing is they tell everybody they are sisters. The guys love it. The two of you must have been raised very "close."

There was this gal that worked at one of the clubs who the guys used to love. When she was on her period, she would lactate. She had four children and breastfed all of them. The doctors said that was the reason for her breasts lactating every month. The guys loved it when she would squirt them. Then you have the guys that ask, "Are any pregnant girls working?"

There is this set of identical twins that run around dressed alike and doing double dances. The guys love them, too. They dress up like cheerleaders. They do look cute, but I have never understood the sister thing with guys. I have a sister and I would never dance or do anything like that with her. It must be a, *twin thing*.

There was this guy who used to come in who liked one of the girls a lot because she would let him suck her toes. He would pay her a lot of money to just suck on her toes all night. He would tell her to go into the back and wash her feet so he would have "nice clean toes to suck on." Let's just say this girl had no class. She would go into the back of our dressing room and run around the dirty bathroom floor barefoot. Then put her feet into the toilet and then take her nasty feet to him. He would suck on her toes after she did that. Can you believe that? To this day, I still don't think he knows what she did or still does. Watch out, toe suckers; it just may be you!

I had this guy another time, during the rodeo, that *loved* to smell my breath and rub my feet. What an interesting combination. He wanted me to dance right in his face, and then after twenty minutes he would want me to sit in the chair across from him while he massaged my feet. The whole breath thing was just a little weird, but the foot massage was incredible. How cool is that they are paying you to rub your feet while you sit there. It doesn't get any better than that.

I remember this time dancing for this guy from Houston. When he started to rub my back, he said something to himself and started to laugh. I was like, "What's so funny?" He said, "My wife asks me to massage her all the time. I do, maybe a third of the time. Here, I just met you and I want to touch you and massage you. I feel so guilty. I never massage her and here I am massaging you." We laughed, but I really don't think he thought it to be funny. His poor wife never gets massaged because he's out massaging strippers.

One quick way I could mesmerize the guys was by singing to them. I have quite the voice and the men love to be serenaded. You could get anything you wanted from these guys once they were under your spell. These men will spend thousands before they realize what just happened. Then again, we all know when a man enters a strip club only one head works right, and it isn't the one with the brain.

I had a customer that used to come in from Idaho to see me all the time. He loved to brush my hair. Once again, he would pay me to sit in his lap while he brushed my hair. I have long, waist-length hair. The guys seem to love it while I am dancing for them especially, when it falls onto their faces as I am dancing.

I had this man approach me one night and ask for a dance. This guy was seven-feet-two-inches tall. The man was almost two feet taller than me. We went against the wall and waited for the next song to start. When I started to dance, he started to get excited. His member started growing down his leg. Halfway down this man's thigh I was starting to freak out. I turned to him and said' "Oh my." He started to laugh and said, "It's not done yet!" By the time it was done, it was all the way down his thigh to his knee. I have never in my life ever felt anything so enormous. He admitted to me it was fifteen inches long. There is no way he could have ever fully put that into a woman. He admitted that he never tried, because most the time they can't even handle half. He said he has to hold it straight with both hands while doing a woman so it doesn't bend.

Could you imagine having something so huge and it basically being *useless*? He said he wished it a little smaller so he didn't encounter so many problems with women when they see it for the first time. "Most are scared of it." He has to ease them into the idea and let them know he won't hurt them. He said, "Most extra large condoms only fit halfway when on." I told him he should be in Porn or some type of freak show with a thing that huge. We just laughed.

Here is another story about how one moment can change your life forever. There was a group of guys who use to come into the club every week after work. They would never get dances, but would try to sell the girl's cars or mortgage insurance or whatever they had to sell. One of the guys was real weird. I asked what his issue was. They tell him to tell me the Mardi Gras story. I looked at him and told him that I wanted to hear the story. I'm curious about things like this. He tells me how he and his wife decided one year to vacation and have a second honeymoon.

They took their vacation during the week of Mardi Gras. The parties down on old town used to get pretty wild. They were drunk that night and got separated in the crowd. The crowds were so deep and thick. When he couldn't find her, he really started to get worried. Then out of nowhere, this beautiful woman grabs him and pulls him down an alleyway. Without saying a word, he follows her around a corner and into a small hotel room. As soon as they entered, she pushed him up against the wall and started to kiss him. He was so mesmerized by this woman. She had a mask on and this long stunning velvet gown.

She kisses him working her way down his neck and unbuttoned his shirt. He was in such shock over what was happening, he said that all he could do was just stand there and let this woman do what she wanted. She then unbuckled his belt and unzipped his pants. He said his eyes rolled back in his head; it was the fastest orgasm he ever had. "The way she touched and massaged me as she sucked my member was phenomenal." He said it was the best blowjob he ever received. Then he said, "It's my turn," and bent her over to dive on in. He said he was so drunk at this point, he was just enjoying the moment. When they were finished, he asked the girl to remove her mask so he could see her face.

He said, "You can only imagine the look on my face when I found out the beautiful women I had just had sex with was a *man*. My buzz was instantly gone. The first thought in my mind was to kill this guy. Then I realized it was the best sex I ever had. No woman had ever made me feel the way he did. When I bent her over, I just assumed she liked it in the butt, when that's where she asked me to put it. I know it's hard to believe someone could be so drunk they couldn't tell the difference between a man and a woman. But it really was hard to tell and he really was a very beautiful woman." I think my jaw was on the floor right about now. This was one of the most shocking stories I think I ever heard. Not many people would be willing to admit to a story like that.

Now the guy and his wife are divorced because he has decided he likes boys better than girls. Fifteen years of marriage, two kids, and he leaves his wife to be with another man. You hear stories all the time of women leaving their husbands for another woman, but this was a first for me.

The reason for telling these stories is to show how diverse the lifestyles are in Vegas. If you don't fit in where you live, I guarantee you will fit in here. Whatever you choose to be or want to be can be done in Vegas. Nobody has to hide who they are, and they don't. You can be whatever you want to be and nobody cares. For Nevada to be a Republican state, the lifestyles are very "liberal."

6

Behind the Make-up and Costumes

This is the chapter that gives the "tell all" about what happens in the locker rooms after the dancing is over and it's time to go home. What do dancers *really* think of the men that they dance for? Not all have the same feelings, but this should relate to a lot. Not all clubs are like the ones in Vegas. Some are dives; others are the finest in the world. I have worked in California, Dallas, Hawaii, Japan, New York, Reno, and Las Vegas. I have seen many different clubs with many different rules and how the girls find their ways to work around the rules. This is the inside stuff. This is the stuff that every man and woman wants to know about a stripper's life.

The girls try to get away with breaking every rule there is to break. Some clubs have six-inch rules; others have three-foot rules. I have even heard of some clubs having six-foot rules. The girls will wear long gowns with g-strings that barely cover their "cookies," and when they bend over they slide their gown and g-string to the side so the men can see everything. They haven't realized they can make more money by not showing anything. If they're not able to show their breasts, they will bend over and pull their outfits down so the guys can see right in. I watched this one girl wear her outfit above her breasts so that when she put her stomach up to the guys face, her breasts were right above his face. One manager came out and yelled at one of the girls for letting the guys suck on her nipples. She informed her, "Her nipple in a guy's mouth was not properly covered." They will do anything to make a buck. Or you get these girls who will let the customer suck on their breasts while they are dancing for the guy. You can hear the guy making sucking noises next to you. I will usually move to a different chair so my customer doesn't think, it's okay to do that. Or the girls will get on all fours and put their butt in the guy's face and then adjust her thong. When a dancer does this move, it allows the guy to see her butt hole. Most of the guys love this. That's how they know they have a nasty dancer. Most of the girls who do this come from nude clubs. They have no problem exposing everything because that is what they are used to: flashing the guy, or walking around with their "cookie lips" hanging out of their g-strings. Some wear the g-strings that are so tiny and barely cover their butt holes. Most don't cover and the girls count on that to expose their "cookies" so the guys will want more dances from them.

When you work in a small club and the girls are all competing for the same money, they can be ruthless. Catty most of the time, others are downright mean. They will start rumors about you. They will start the rumor about you with a customer. I remember this time a year after this girl had been dancing at the club. We were all laughing about the rumor that was going around about her "doing the manager." He was old and we all knew it was a lie. One of the girls pops out with, "I started that rumor because I didn't like you when you first started dancing here." They started laughing and hugged each other.

I was always one to mind my own business. One night, walking into the club, this girl says to me, "Where's your VIP glass?" I looked at her and said, "I just walked in." She said, "I thought they just handed the glass and money to you when you walked through the door?" I was so mad that this girl I didn't even know was paying attention to how much money I made. It shows how the girls are catty and pay too much attention to other girls instead of concentrating on themselves.

Most girls hate the job and can't wait to get out of school to stop. Others do it to raise kids and to pay the bills. Many do it to pay for drug habits, or to support useless boyfriends. I personally loved the job, but after several years I got tired of grinding on men and having men disrespect me. They would manhandle me and treat me like a paid object. I am paid for, but they don't have the right to grope me or hurt me. They try to hold me down against them and hold my hips so they can grind me real hard, or so I can't move. Or they lock their arms around me so that I can't move. Guys, don't do this; it only makes us defensive and it won't get you a very good dance

One little club where I worked had a power outage one day. The guys didn't want to leave the bar and we girls wanted to stay and wait for the power to come back on. So, we opened all of the exit doors for light and one of the guys had a portable stereo in his car. He brought it in and we still danced on stage for tips and had fun for a couple of hours. We told jokes and everyone showed what stupid human trick they could do. One of the girls was lighting matches on her nipples. Then another girl pops out with the funniest story. Now this was when you could still smoke in the California bars. She had this guy who was a jerk at her stage. She said all she could think about was getting down on all fours in front of him and backing her butt up to his face. Then, wait for him to light a smoke and pass gas right when he has the lighter to his face. She said,

"Could you imagine his expression as he got torched?" She said she had always dreamed of doing that to some drunken jerk. We all laughed so hard we were crying. Picture it, some stripper on all fours with her butt backed up to some guy and she rips one right in his face as he lights his smoke. The Flaming Stripper, now that would be funny.

I went to dance in Japan for a month with some friends. They allow full masturbation on stage and the more you get into your performance, the more money you could make. The girls would line up on the stage and compete for the guy's attention. The more you fingered yourself and bent over and opened everything up, the more money you would make. I couldn't do it. I was home in two days. In most clubs, pretty much anything goes. For American money, the girls will do anything you want. You can get anything sexual done to you for any price in Japan and the outlying areas. I was once told that they sell their "virginal daughters" to rich businessmen to "pop their cherries." Once their cherries have been popped, they are sent to dance in the clubs to make money for their families. One of the nastier girls made $30,000 that month. I had another friend dance there for five years and then was able to retire. She now owns several pizza parlors.

Some of my friends from Brazil who came to dance in Vegas told me about the clubs there. When you walk inside, they hand you a robe. You then proceed to a room where you change into the robe and then return to the main floor. The girls will then dance for you completely nude. They will rub all over you and purposely make your robe slip to the side. Then they proceed to ask "if you want to go further to finish what you started." They take you into a private booth and anything goes for the right price. That's why my friends came to the States to dance. The dancing there is more of a brothel than a dance club. I have also heard the same thing about the clubs in Europe. You walk in and they give you a locker key and they hand you a towel. You take all your clothes off and walk around with the towel around you. My customer said, "It's more like a spa than a dance club." You find the girl you want and then go to a private booth. Anything goes. You just have to settle on a price. I heard they are very desperate for money and will do anything for fifty dollars per half hour. Now I understand why a lot of foreign girls come to the states to dance.

One thing that really bothered me about being a dancer was how I was received when someone found out I was a stripper. The way people judge you because you are a dancer. Most have the perception we are all hookers or stupid, and that's why we take off our clothes for a living. We have "sexual issues" or were "molested as a child." I was never molested as a child, and I am far from being stupid. I can't stand people who judge you on the basis of your profession. I am a dancer. If I wanted to be a hooker, I could go work in a brothel. There is a big difference between the two and people need to understand that. You can pay any girl to leave a club for the right price, but that is the dancer's own personal decision. I was offered $10,000 from a French director to go back to his suite. The offer was very tempting, but not worth crossing the line for me. I like the person I see in the mirror every morning. One girl I worked with really did have sexual issues. I don't know her past, but she loved to dance really nasty and would do two-for-one dances for the guys. If she came to work and found out the cops were there undercover, she would leave knowing her dances would get her fired, or worse, arrested.

You have to be careful with what you say to a customer. You never know who is going to be an undercover cop. If you agree to meet a customer after hours, or agree to an amount of money for "sex," you can be arrested and charged with solicitation. They take your work card and you can no longer work in this town. The under covers are in the clubs often and usually pick major holiday weekends to solicit the girls. A lot of girls come into town from out of state and don't know how they work. It makes them easy targets to solicit since they are, for the most part, naïve. Never agree to leave for any amount of money for any reason and you will never have a thing to worry about. I said earlier in one chapter that I would go gambling with some customers. Yes, I could have been cited for solicitation. I would only agree to meet a customer outside of the club if he had been in to see me several times. Only if I knew the guy was not a cop.

Then there is the issue of girls stealing from each other. Dancers are bigger thieves than any person I have ever met. I don't know if it's the greed, or what. I haven't quite figured it out, yet. I had a locker at the first club I started working at. I used to find money missing out of my locker, daily. Sometimes it was small amounts; other times it was a lot. After three days of money missing, I started carrying a purse to hold my money and I never lost it again.

About a year after I had moved to Vegas, another girl was getting her money stolen the same way mine was. She called the cops. She had them fingerprint her locker to see if prints would come up, and they did. The girl had been removing the screws out of the hinges and opening the lockers backwards. It was this girl who had been accusing another girl all along. Funny how life works that way? She was arrested and charged with theft.

Some of the girls in the smaller clubs are so bad about stealing money, make-up, and costumes. If you don't keep your stuff locked up, it will be gone before you know it. I buy the expensive make-up for myself and leave it at home. Then carry a small case to work with me that has the touch up make-up so they won't steal it. If it's not a name brand, they will leave it alone. One girl had her outside clothes and shoes stolen from her while she was working. She had to wear her stripper clothes home that night.

There was this time this chick was real drunk and got the brilliant idea to bring bolt cutters to work and cut locks off of lockers to steal the girls money. I couldn't believe the nerve of this girl. She had these damn bolt cutters that were two feet long and walking down the locker isles cutting off locks and stealing the girl's money. She was fired and then arrested.

Another big thing with the girls is that if they like your outfit, or are jealous of you in it, they will try to ruin it. I have seen girls dump drinks on another girl to ruin her outfit. Even seen others burn holes in the girl's clothes and the girl not even know they are being burned. You can still smoke in the clubs in Vegas, so it's very easy to burn someone's outfit if you don't like them. I've seen it many times. I have even been witness to a girl smashing gum into another girl's hair because she made her mad. There were several witnesses to the incident, and they were more than willing to talk to get this girl fired for her bad attitude. It's like working with a bunch of grammar school girls.

When you start working in the little clubs, they don't have many amenities for the girls. You basically had to take your own lunch or dinner to work with you. If you worked two shifts, they would allow you to go out for an hour for dinner. Otherwise, they would have a couple of vending machines and that's about it. It was nice to make the move to Vegas where they care about their girls. Most of the clubs have moms that work in the locker rooms for us. Some clubs offer great food and moms that cook; others don't. One of the clubs in Vegas had this mom that would cook the most incredible meals. Everything she would make would be homemade and good. It was total "*Grandma food*."

The fun thing about being in the back room with all the girls is you get to see all of the best and worst that plastic surgery has to offer. Everybody always swears their doctor is the best. I have seen some real butcher jobs, where the girl's nipples pointed off in different directions. I think we all know what I am talking about: headlights are not even. Some aren't so bad; others are so horrible I would sue the doctor that did it. One of the girls had gone in for a facelift. She had to do a whole new hairstyle to cover the doctor's mistake. Please, make sure you check your doctor out completely before you let them take a knife to your body. One of the biggest mistakes made by girls is going by price, rather than whether or not the doctor is good. You get what you pay for!

One of the funny things about having a huge dressing room with showers and lockers is that most of the dancers will walk around naked. They will go into the eating area naked and sit down to eat. The house moms usually yell at them to get dressed while in their kitchen. But it's very funny to see girls sitting to eat topless or completely nude. I even saw a girl change her tampon at the dinner table one night. Like I said, some have class and others have none. Or we get the girls who will come in and change their clothes right in front of us while we are eating. They bend over and just expose themselves for all to see while we eat. Not quite what I want to look at while eating. No manners!

Other times the girls are so drunk that they are in the back locker rooms licking each other's "cookies," or just fondling each other. Most dancers are very touchy with each other and see nothing wrong with rubbing another girl's breast or butt if it will make the sale. Others like to leave work and go out "booty hunting." They get so worked up at work that they go out on the hunt after work to find a boy to fulfill their needs. Most dancers are very sexual people and have no problem letting a man know if she wants them. We use our bodies to get what we want at work and for fun. That is why guys love to date dancers. They tend to be more sexually open than most other women.

The more upscale clubs in Vegas really take care of their girls. The better clubs offered lockers, showers, sauna, and tanning beds. You could tan for free, so the girls stayed tan all year long. Others offered services such as a manicurist, a make-up artist, and hairdressers. Some clubs have built-in costume shops for the girls. It used to be just a couple of shops downtown were the places where you found your clothes. Now, the clubs have the shops built right in.

I have seen some catfights in the back room. Sometimes when the girls get drunk, problems do occur. They have fights over customers, girls trying to steal another girl's customer. Other times, it's because they are fighting over what they got paid. There was this one time these two sisters who danced had issues over a customer. It started out with them yelling at each other. Then it went to slapping and, from there, to shoe-throwing. We all ran out of the dressing room. Can you imagine someone throwing a hooker shoe at you? These things have six-inch stiletto heels. It could seriously be considered a deadly weapon. They are throwing these things at each other and shattering the mirrors on the walls. The bouncers had to make their way into the room and pry them apart. It had to be the most aggressive fight between women I have ever seen. Fighting is not allowed and usually the girls will be fired for it.

I was in the VIP room one night when, a few tables over, a Russian gal sat with a customer. She was obviously a racist, and she had no idea there was an African-American girl sitting right behind her. She said something, the music stopped, and we all heard the word "nigger" pop out of her mouth. The African-American girl stood up, took her beer bottle, and cracked it over the Russian girl's head. She hit her across the forehead. Blood started to shoot everywhere. She was rushed to the hospital and had several stitches in her head. She was fired and the African-American girl was able to keep her job.

Here is a nasty story. This one is not for the weak. There was a night I was working and it was very late. I was standing in the back room waiting to use the restroom when this girl comes running up screaming that she needs to use the bathroom. There is a line of six girls and we all have to use the restroom pretty bad. Nobody would let this girl cut. She was standing in the middle of the bathroom, freaking out. You could tell she was extremely drunk and was definitely on something else. She was holding her legs crossed when all of a sudden she screamed, "Oh my," and poop started shooting everywhere. The thong up her butt made it shoot out both sides and down her legs. It has got to be one of the most disgusting things I have ever witnessed. There this girl stood in the middle of the bathroom floor pooping herself. We all ran out of the bathroom quickly. She definitely knew how to clear the line.

I have danced for a lot of years and I have to say this about women. When you are around them on a constant basis, it's real easy to see how they live. They clog up the toilets with their drug folds. They throw their soiled tampons on the floor or behind the toilet. They pee all over the toilet seats, and all over the floors. I thought men were bad at hygiene, but they have nothing on women. Some of these girls can be so disgusting and nasty. Most don't even wash their hands after using the restroom. Think about that the next time you let some stripper stick her finger in your mouth. Also, when a gal sits on your lap and the smell of her perfume overwhelms you, the reason is because they don't wash their outfits every night, so they smell like smoke. They spray lots of perfume to cover up the body odor and smoke smell.

Some really gross things have happened over the years that I have been dancing. One thing that has happened, to a lot girls that I have witnessed is "the dreaded tampon string" sticking out of your g-string, or worse, sticking out of you at a nude club. The next few stories deal with this issue.

There was this girl I danced with when I first started. She was a very nice person and had a great personality. The guys loved her from the very first day she started working. She was getting ready one night for stage, and she forgot to tuck her string into her g-string. She went on stage to do her performance. When she went to take her shorts off that's when we all saw it. She was bent over to the crowd and there it was, glowing in the dark from the black lights, her tampon string. One of the other gals ran up and told her. She ran off stage and into the locker room. She waited for the bar to close that night to leave. She stayed in the locker room all night for fear of facing everyone who had witnessed her embarrassing stage performance. I felt so bad for her. You know, she never came back to the club again.

This other girl I danced with told me about her tampon string story and this one is got to be the worst. Talk about being embarrassed. She went to the nude club here in town and asked to work. They hired her and she worked that night. She was a very pretty girl and had a hot Body. She went to do her stage performance that night and, in the middle of her routine, she grabbed the pole, hiked her legs straight up into the air, and spread them as wide as she could. Then she looked down and noticed her tampon string sticking straight out of her "cookie." She was like, "What the hell was I supposed to do? Reach down and stuff the thing back in? There it was, like an arrow, sticking straight out of me. I thought I had tucked it in, but I guess I hadn't." She said she closed her legs, walked off stage, got her clothes, and left. She never went back to that bar again. Personally, I have never had this happen to me because it's one of my biggest fears as a dancer, to be dancing for some guy and bend over and see your tampon string hanging out.

It is funny to hear the girls talk about it happening to them. I have seen it happen to girls on stage as they are sitting on stage thinking they are sexy when they spread their legs, and people see this glow in the dark string hanging out of them. It has got to be one of the most embarrassing things that can happen to a stripper.

The funny thing about being on your period is that it's like the men can smell the "bitch in heat" a mile away. Just like a male dog, they are so attracted to you. It's like you put off some type of chemical that creates a sort of chemical reaction in them. I would love for a doctor to let me know if this is what is really happening to men when around a woman on her period. I tended to make more money that week than during any other week of the month.

There are several things men do in the clubs that can really make a dancer mad or gross her out. One of the few things I can't stand is when you are dancing for a guy and he sticks his tongue out at you and makes sick gestures with it. They do this as you are dancing for them, or they try to lick your breasts if you get too close. You just turn your back on these guys and don't look at them for the rest of the dance. You don't even ask for another dance; you just get your money and go. Honestly, does a man think by making those sick gestures with his tongue we are going to want him? I don't understand what is going through his mind at that very moment when they stick their tongue out at you. Another of my pet peeves is when they try to stick their tongue in your ear. Why would you want to stick your tongue in the ear of a girl you don't know? The worst is when they try to kiss and lick all over your neck and back. I have had men lick the whole top of my shoulders from side to side. Then I run into the back and wash off as soon as possible. Men, don't do this. It's disgusting.

Then there are the girls you aren't quite sure are girls. Over the years of dancing, I have seen plenty of "he/she's" that have danced. The one sure way to tell is the Adam's apple. You see these girls that are absolutely beautiful and then you look at her neck then you aren't so sure it's a girl. I have seen some that have actually done the "tuck thing" with their really small man parts and get away with it. The guys actually think it's a woman. It scares me to think most men wouldn't be able to tell the difference in the dark of the strip clubs. A customer actually asked me, "Why do they keep it so dark?" My reply was, "So you can't see what's really dancing for you." If the guys could see some of these girls in the light, they would run out of the club screaming for their lives. Not to be mean, but some of these girls really should not be dancing.

Every now and then in the upscale clubs, the owners would clean house, meaning if they thought you had gained too much weight, you were warned to lose it or lose your job. Or they will just send you to the morning shift. Nobody wants to work the morning shift. You have the drunken leftovers from the night girls and it's never crowded in the mornings. It's very hard to earn a living on the morning shift. I remember one time I was walking with a friend and the owner walked by and said, "Damn, are we paying them by the pound?" about my friend. She was fired and I never saw her again. If the boss thought your butt was getting to big, he would make comments about it and that was your warning. Then again, dancers make so much money doing this job; isn't it worth keeping? It takes all kinds to make up the stripper world. There has to be someone for everyone. Over the years, I have danced with several women who were over the age of forty. There were even a few that were young grandmothers. They had their kids at a young age and their kids are repeating them. There was a mother and daughter who used to dance together at one of the clubs where I worked.

Having said all of this, the girls *do* deserve to have some good said about them at the end. Some dancers are pigs; others out there (like me) do it for the money and to raise kids. Dancers are a very tight-knit group when it comes to their own. When a dancer is in trouble, you can count on the other dancers to step up and help out. One of the girls had a problem with her baby. It was born premature. The girls all stepped up and donated money to help her and her husband when they needed it. Another girl was murdered and the girls all donated money for the cost of the funeral. I have let some girls borrow money and have been paid back. Others just blow you off, and you learn they are the flakes in the business. I give credit to the good girls of the occupation and wish them all the luck in the world. For those who trash their lives and don't think the money will ever end *good luck* (because you are going to need it).

I saved my money and used it to open my own business. Now, I travel when I want and go on vacation when I want. I get paid for doing another job I truly love and it's incredible. Dancing gave me everything I have and I thank the business for that. Girls, save your money and do something more with your life. Don't be the fifty-year-old stripper working the morning shift wondering what happened to her life.

All names have been left out, to protect the guilty.

0-595-33176-9

Printed in the United States
47982LVS00005B/300